# Crackers and Milk

*Thanks for Reading*

by Arlene Nelson

*arlene nelson*

## *Acknowledgments*

I wish to express my sincere thanks to my editor, Char Valters, and my proofreader, Joy McComb, without whose help and expertise this book would not have been published. I will always appreciate their skill and patience.

Thanks also to my husband, Bob, and my children and grandchildren, especially Patty and Jason, who pushed me and inspired me to move ahead with my book.

And at the end of this writing, editing and proofreading process, the editor and publisher of the *Minnesota Memories* book series, Joan Claire Graham, enabled me go to press by doing layout, cover design, pre-press editing and photo preparation. Thanks again to all these people.

Photo on page 81 used with permission from the Orphanage Museum, Owatonna, Minnesota

# CRACKERS AND MILK
## by Arlene Nelson

*Behold the Works of the Old---*
*Let your Heritage not be lost,*
*But bequeath it as a Memory,*
*Treasure and Blessing---*
*Gather the lost and the hidden*
*And preserve it for thy Children.*

*Christian Metz, 1846*
*Founder of the Amana Colonies in Iowa*

## AUTHOR'S NOTES:

*In the beginning there was Ireland, the land of the green! But there was a time, around the 1850s, when a great famine came upon the land. It was a time of great hardships, and people struggled trying to farm and raise a family. At that time a young lad named G. F. (Hiram) McCooke lived with his family on a small homestead about 12 miles east of Galway Bay. The only story that was handed down from this generation was about Hiram's sister, Kathlena, who was killed while walking home from school with him. There was a terrible rainstorm with hail the size of a ball, Hiram would tell, and she was beaten and injured so badly by the hail that she did not survive. Hiram would tell that Kathlena lay on top of him to protect him, and she died a heroine.*

*It became common practice during those hard times for young boys, at the age of 12, to be sent out into the world to fend for themselves. Hiram was given a small sack with three potatoes and sent on his way. He ended up on a farm nearby, working for a farmer who had a large herd of dairy cattle. Legend tells of the master selling some of his herd to a dealer in America, and one stipulation of the deal was that the herd would arrive at their destination, Dubuque, Iowa, alive and well. Dubuque had large stockyards where the cattle were eventually sold to pioneers settling in the area.*

*The farmer offered Hiram a free one-way trip to America if he would tend to his cattle on the ship and see to it that they were fed and cared for so they would stay alive until they arrived at Dubuque. The trip took about six weeks. The ship went from Galway Bay through the Gulf of Mexico, then north up the Mississippi River to Davenport, Iowa. Hiram was somehow successful in his endeavor, and started a new life in and around the stockyards of Dubuque. When he put in for his papers to stay in America, the authorities changed his last name to Cook.*

**William Cook**

*It was told that Hiram married at a very young age (some say 15) to a pretty young bride who was also 15. How many children were born of this marriage remains unclear, but it is known that one son, William Cook, was born. William married Etta Schueman (her name at the time of her death), Caroline and Della were born of this union. Caroline married Windsor Richards, and they had four children before they separated. Their names were Sarah, Edythe, William (Billy) and Windsor Jr.*

*Windsor Sr. also fathered a child named Violet, who was born of Della, Caroline's sister. Caroline and Windsor took this child in and raised her as their own. Della was very young when she gave birth, probably around 12, and was "simple minded," the folks would tell.*

**Caroline and Windsor Richards' wedding photo: November 10, 1910**

**Crackers and Milk** *is the story of Caroline and Windsor's oldest child, Sarah Etta Richards, born in a cabin in the countryside near the town of Clear Lake, Iowa, close by the Clear Lake on March 16, 1912. Sarah eventually grew to hate her name, so all of her adult life was called "Sally."*

*This is the story of Sally as I imagine it to be from the stories she related to me at different times during her life. She would sit and reminisce for hours while at her treadle sewing machine mending and constructing clothing for her five children. Sometimes she would only express tears and tales of woe. Sometimes she would just talk of one instance for a few minutes and then become quiet. Other times she would become very angry and relate over and over again some of the horrors she had endured. I would hear about her childhood when we were working in the garden, when we were doing chicken chores, when we were washing dishes together. She would ramble on when we were resting on the porch steps together waiting for the kitchen floor to dry after washing it on our hands and knees.*

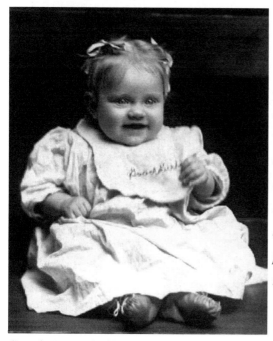

*Often, as I grew older, I would say, "Mom, tell me one of your stories." And, if she was in the mood, she would start to talk—some weepy tales; others loud, angry, and harsh chapters of her life. Once in a while, but not often, she would tell a joyous story about a new pair of shoes or finding a nest with baby bunnies in it.*

**Sarah Etta "Sally" Richards, 10 months**

*It is now time to put all these stories and tales together. I will try to relate her life, as it must have been, to my children and grandchildren so they will never forget where and how the legacy of their heritage started. I want to pass along the stories of her early years as Sarah, but I would never want them to forget Grandma Sally as they knew her.*

*She was a fun-loving grandma with a great sense of humor who loved her children and grandchildren with all her heart. Sally often vowed that her children would never have to grow up experiencing any of the trials and tribulations that she went through. She was married more than 53 years to her faithful husband, Edgar Percy Sanborn, and they had five children: Paul, Eugene, Arlene, James, and Shirley. I am Arlene Pearl (Sanborn) Nelson.*

***1950 Sanborn Family Photo:***
***Front Row:  Edgar, Shirley, Sally***
***Back: Paul with wife Arlene, Eugene, Arlene Sanborn Nelson, James***

## *Chapter 1*
## *Two Babies and a Buggy*

*This is Sally's story.*

The very first memories I have stored in my mind are those of anguish and chaos. I was put on my folks' bed with my younger brother Billy, and sister Edythe, and told to stay there in the dark of the night. I remember hearing cries and loud voices coming from the other side of the curtained door. We started to cry, but Mommy would come into our room to tell us that everything was going to be okay and that very soon we were going to have a new baby sister or brother. *This was the little baby girl to be named Violet, born of Della, Caroline's sister.* Not long after that, it was time for Mommy to have her new baby. He came in the night too! They named him Windsor.

*Sarah, Billy and Edythe, taken in Iowa in 1915*

My next vivid memory came soon after that when I was in the kitchen, a small noisy room, with many people gathered closely together. There were loud, angry voices, and suddenly a total stranger ripped me away from my mother's leg! A blanket was thrown over my head, and I, along with Edythe, Billy, Violet, and baby Windsor, were rushed to a waiting buggy outside. It was cold, windy, and rainy, and we were terribly frightened.

*The record shows that Sarah and her siblings were entered into the Iowa Soldiers' Home in Davenport on March 15, 1919. Sarah was barely 7, Edythe 6, Billy 4, Violet 2, and Windsor almost 6 months.*

We were taken to a large building where we were housed with many other children and separated from one another. I remember wandering down long, cold halls in the dark of night looking for my brothers and sisters. I was always found, spanked, and put back into my bed with my hands tied to the bedpost to keep me from wandering again.

I also recollect being sat down at a long table with many other kids. Then some lady would bring around bowls and slam them down in front of us. Someone else would come behind with soda crackers. She would break up a handful and drop them in my bowl. Then a third person would come behind me with a big pitcher filled with milk and proceed to fill the bowl with milk. I remember this being my supper every single night I was at this place. I learned to love this flavorful concoction and have treated myself to crackers and milk just about every single day of my life.

*Edythe, Violet, Windsor, Billy and Sarah, 1919*

The next memory I have is looking over a high crib-style bed at my baby brother, Windsor. My eyes could barely peek over the top of the mattress. They had brought all of us kids into the room. I remember Mommy and Dad coming in the door rather abruptly and ignoring the rest of us kids to rush to the baby's crib. Mommy was screaming and crying! Other folks were there, too, crying and talking as they looked down on the sleeping baby. I heard someone say, "Your baby Windsor is gone!" Gone . . . ? He was right there sleeping! Couldn't they see? But they told us kids that he was dead, and soon Jesus would come and take him home to heaven! Then I cried too! I remember saying something like, "Take him to heaven? Why not just give him to my mother? She would make him well! She would give him milk from her titty, and he would be all right. I just know it"! They all cried even harder then.

My little sister Violet was very confused. She had been born deaf and couldn't understand anything that was happening, only the chaos and confusion. All she could do was scream and tug on Mommy's dress, begging to be picked up. My brother Billy, frail and weak, cowered in the corner. He had "fits," what we now call epileptic seizures, every hour or so. He was delirious most of the time with all the confusion. When they tried to take him out of the room Dad put up an awful fuss and insisted that we be left alone as a family to say good-bye to Windsor. He held Billy to quiet him. It was then that everyone left except our family. We all cried because we were so happy to see Mommy again, to touch her, to smell the soap on her dress, and to feel her hand on our backs patting us so we could quit crying.

## Chapter 2
## *She Never Looked Back*

Somehow we were returned to our folks from that terrible Soldiers' Home to our little cabin. Mommy was never the same after that. She sat on the edge of the bed and cried for long periods of time. I think she was terribly sad over losing Windsor. We tried to get her to play with us and help us get something to eat, but she couldn't seem to handle anything. We had to pull up a chair to fill the wood stove with kindling to start the fire to try to warm ourselves and fix something to eat. I remember trying to make the paring knife work so I could cut potatoes into the pan for frying. We just ate them raw most of the time.

Mommy had taught Edythe and me how to milk a cow early on in life, and she would send us out into the clearing when she heard a cowbell. We would try our best to milk one or two of the cows to fill our little lard can, but first we filled our bellies with warm fresh milk directly from the cow. Our faces and dresses got soaked. Then we would bring the milk back for the family to drink and beg our dad, when he was home, to bring us crackers from town so we could have our crackers and milk just like what we had eaten in that awful home. We showed Mommy how to fix them in a bowl, and after that we ate as many meals as there were crackers for.

Dad was gone for long periods of time. I remember him being home only occasionally, and when he did come home, he always brought whiskey with him. Sooner or later he and Mommy would start screaming and fighting, and he would beat on her something terrible. Then he left again. The only person who ever came to check on us was a man from town. He said he was a minister, and he and Mommy talked for a long time about Windsor. I remember playing in the woods trying to find berries while they visited.

Once in a while Mommy would bake biscuits for us. Those were the times when she must have been feeling better. I will never forget the smell and taste of her warm baked biscuits. And sometimes Dad would bring home something for us to eat. We never knew where it came from or even what it was, but we ate it anyway. At least we knew we weren't going to have to go to bed hungry that night.

Mommy often went away in the evenings after dark when Dad was gone. She would put us in bed and tell us not to get out. We would fall asleep all huddled together, crying, because we were afraid to stay alone.

Then came the day when she told us kids to go outside and stay there. "I will tell you when to come back in," she said. "If you wait long enough you are going to see our new baby." We were so excited about another baby! _Records show that the "visitor" fathered this child._ Mommy named her Dorothy. I remember she had a lot of black hair. She looked so different because the rest of us had auburn red hair.

"Such a pretty baby, but she sure cries a lot," Edythe would say. I was so happy that Mommy had a new little baby to hold and love, as I knew Windsor was never coming back. Now she wouldn't be sad anymore. But she was still quiet and downcast, even after baby Dorothy came.

Finally, one morning, Mommy got up really early. She didn't know it, but she woke me when she went to take a whimpering baby Dorothy out of bed. She picked her up ever so carefully and wrapped her in her blanket as she quietly turned and stepped out the door closing it ever so gently. I got up and tiptoed over to the window of the cabin. I stood on a chair and stretched to look out that window. I will never forget that scene as long as I live. She simply meandered through the clearing around our cabin with baby Dorothy in her arms, walking slowly into the trees, onto the path and out of sight. She never looked back. We were alone, the four of us: Edythe, age 6, Billy, age 4 with epileptic seizures, Violet, age 3 and deaf, and me, age 7.

*The story goes that Caroline took baby Dorothy back to Rockton, Illinois, to live with her mother, Etta Cook. She divorced Windsor Richards and married the baby's father.*

I figured Mommy would come back soon so we ate our mush that she had left on the stove. We kept busy playing all day, but when evening came, she still hadn't returned. We went to bed thinking she had walked to town and would be home in the morning. It was about 27 years before I had contact with my mother and Dorothy again.

*Sarah, Billy, Edythe and Violet, 1920*

# *Chapter 3*
# *Ollie and the Trunk*

We were left alone until Dad came home again. When he found out that our mother had walked away with Dorothy, he told us not to worry. He was going back to town to get us another mother. Once again we were left alone, but he did come back with a new girl named Ollie. Ollie was a young girl about 16 years old. She walked with a terrible limp on her right side and bounced up and down with every step she took. She had been brutally beaten as a young child. We laughed at her when we saw her coming down the path. We told her she looked funny walking that way, and she laughed right along with us.

She seemed so happy to come to live with us. She smiled and laughed at everything we youngsters did or said and even played outdoors with us! She taught us how to play "Button-Button–Who's Got the Button." We played that a lot when it was raining and we had to stay in the cabin. It was good to have someone around again who would take care of us. But one night Dad came home drunk and mad. He started to throw things around, hollering about those people coming to take us kids away once again!

The next thing I remember is running back and forth in the dark with things from the house and handing them to Dad and Ollie, who were in the back of a wagon. I remember how we struggled to load our mother's trunk that her mother had given her for a wedding gift. Dad insisted we take it along so we could keep things in it.

***Our mother's trunk***

The wagon looked somewhat like the covered wagons you see in the museums today, but the sides were higher. Dad had covered the wood with creosote to preserve it, which stank terribly. And there was some sort of canvas cover over the top. We hurriedly carried out everything that Ollie and Dad wanted. I remember Ollie crying when she came out of the house. I think it was because we had to leave our dog, Pepper, behind. Dad said we couldn't take him because he would bark all the time. All of us kids started to cry then. We did get to take our kitty, Witty, along. We left rather quietly but quickly in the middle of the night. Ollie said not to lock the door because if we kids ever came back we wouldn't have a key to get in. I wondered what she meant by that.

We traveled all night until the sun started to come up. Then Dad found a place deep in a woods, where there was nothing but brambles and trees. There he sank into a deep sleep while the rest of us got out and gathered twigs and small branches for Ollie to start a fire. She cooked us mush for breakfast—the best—so sweet and warm in our tummies. After breakfast, Ollie napped on and off all day while Edythe and I played and giggled just like always. We were very close. She was only a year younger than I so we had a lot in common. We could hardly talk fast enough to tell each other everything that was going through our minds.

Edythe and I wondered how our mother would ever find us. How would Pepper get along without us? Where was Dad taking us? When were we going back home? Would those people from that terrible Soldiers' Home find us out here? We were so happy to be away from that awful big place, but we were scared to be out here too! We even wondered what they did with our little brother, Windsor. Did they put him in the ground like they did with the neighbor man down the trail from our cabin? That would be terrible! How would he ever find his way home to heaven? How would Jesus know where to dig to find him and take him to heaven? We cried together under a big old tree on that quiet place with the bright morning sun beginning to shine out under the clouds.

_Records show that Sarah and her siblings were "inmates" of the Iowa Soldiers' Home, an orphanage in Davenport. It is not clear how or why authorities took them from their family. Their case records have been found at the Muscatine, Iowa, Welfare Agency. Sarah believed, until the day she died, that Windsor was buried in the orphanage cemetery in Davenport. Sarah planned a spring trip there with her family to honor his grave site and collect records relating to herself and her siblings. Unfortunately she fell ill in August and passed away in November._

## Chapter 4
### *I'll Bring the Belt*

Dad told us the next day that we were going to travel at night until we got to Minnesota. Edythe and I liked traveling at night because the wagon wiggled and squeaked as it rocked from side to side. It made it easy to fall asleep. But it was hard to stay quiet and hidden during the day when the folks tried to sleep. I had to take Billy away to lie under a tree where he wouldn't get hurt when he had his spells, and I tried to remember to give him water every so often. But keeping track of Violet was another thing. She loved to wander free and seemed to thrive on outside air. It was spring so she constantly took her coat off and lost it somewhere. Then I had to hunt it down. She squealed and made crazy loud noises when she was happy, which always woke up the folks.

Sometimes Dad would come out with his belt, and I would get a couple of whacks for not keeping the other kids quiet. He told me I was big enough and should know better. "Keep those damn kids quiet!" he yelled. "If I hear the dogs barking from the farms, that means you're making too much noise. So you better watch out, Sarah, because the next time I have to come out, I will bring the belt!"

It was really hard to keep the noise down with a little one who was deaf and another who always had those terrible spells. But Edythe and I sure tried. We would lie beside the two of them and read the clouds or tell them funny stories about the many rabbits we saw. We often played "Button-Button–Who's Got the Button." We went for walks nearby to hunt for food, and often we found some kind of berry bush. I tried to eat just one to see if they were any good, but usually they were too bitter or hard to eat. It must have been too early in the spring. But one day Ollie showed us what asparagus looks like. When we found it we sometimes ate it raw, or if there was a lot, Ollie cooked it in water to soften it up. We thought it sure tasted good.

After we got to Minnesota, we started traveling during the day. By this time we had lost our kitten, Witty. She went hunting, but when she hadn't returned when we were ready to leave, Dad wouldn't wait for her. We youngsters bawled for days about that. But what could we do? It was hard for us to sit all day in that stinky, bumpy wagon. Sometimes we were allowed to get out and walk, but it was hard for Edythe and me to keep up with the horses for very long as we walked with bare feet. Violet was too small to keep up, and Billy was too frail to walk very far. Dad hardly ever stopped for anything once he got going. He didn't want to meet any of the people who came along and tried to talk to us. He just tipped his hat and kept going. I guess he was kind of shy or maybe he felt like a stranger and didn't want to make friends. He told us not to talk to anyone either. We stopped for water if we found a pump close to the road. We had a big can to hold the water, but it got old and tasted funny after a while if we didn't empty it often and put in clean water.

We started to eat better when we traveled during the day. Dad went out after dark, and Ollie said he was hunting for food. She said it was the best time to hunt in Minnesota. Somehow, though, we always seemed to go to bed hungry. Sometimes Ollie saved the leftover mush from breakfast, and she fried it for supper . . . but not always. Yet there always seemed to be plenty of fresh eggs or chicken for breakfast.

Even with the fresh eggs and chicken, we still begged Dad to get us milk so we could have our crackers and milk for supper. Ollie had remembered to bring the cracker barrel along. But we had to ration our milk if we wanted crackers and milk, and by this time the cracker barrel was getting close to empty. Once Ollie opened a jar of applesauce she had stored in a box, and we thought we were in heaven that night. She started fixing soda bread or biscuits more in Minnesota too. She said the smell of baked bread was more fragrant in Minnesota than in Iowa. We really feasted when Dad got lucky enough to shoot a pheasant or rabbit. He said he had to count his bullets though, so he didn't do that very often.

It took us all summer to travel wherever it was we were going. I learned, much later in life, that we traveled from near Davenport, Iowa, to Merrifield, Minnesota, which is about thirty miles north of Brainerd, a distance of nearly 350 miles.

I don't remember going through very many towns. Dad always stayed on the outskirts, but he would sometimes sneak into town after dark. Ollie gave him a terrible scolding and talking to when he got back if he had too much liquor on his breath. Then he got very mean, started yelling, and beat on her. Edythe and I begged her to keep quiet so she wouldn't get hurt. Sometimes Ollie lay in the wagon for a couple of days after one of those episodes. Her eyes were all swollen and black, and she hurt terribly. She cried a lot under her breath during those times. I think she was as scared of Dad as we were. He could be an awfully mean, cold-hearted man when he decided to strike out with his hands and belt.

Poor Ollie! I felt sorry for her. She was so skinny. I often told her that I was too full to finish my mush, or that I didn't like my mush anymore so she could eat the rest out of my bowl. I don't know if it helped her get better, but it always made her smile, and then I always got a special hug.

*Windsor Richards and an unidentified passenger are pictured in his covered wagon, with the horses he used to travel from Davenport, Iowa, to Merrifield, Minnesota, with Ollie and four children, a distance of nearly 350 miles.*

## Chapter 5
### *Fetching Water, Fighting Mosquitoes, Finding a Preacher*

I do remember traveling around a town named Owatonna. Dad said that there was no way we were going into that town because it was named after the Indians who lived there. But Dad and Ollie had heard that there was a good place to get water near town and that an Indian princess had been cured of a terrible disease when she drank this special mineral spring water. They talked for a long time about how they could sneak into that part of the woods without being noticed by the Indians. They decided that sending the two older girls would be the best bet. Edythe and I were given the two syrup pails we had used often for getting creek water for Ollie when she needed it. Dad told us to walk toward the woods ahead and look for a path that was bigger than the others. We were to follow it until we heard water splashing. That would be the springs, he thought. We weren't to talk to anyone and were to act like Violet, deaf and dumb, if someone talked to us. And if anyone tried to pick us up, we were to run back into the woods like the devil was after us. We were terrified, but we knew we had to do what Dad said or get another whipping with his belt.

Edythe was braver and more daring so she started along the path and pulled me by the hand. We walked with her pulling me along for quite a ways before I got the courage to take the lead and go in front along the path.

I don't think Edythe was ever afraid of anything. How could she not fear strangers? My God—look what they had done to us back home! I worried about these Indians. Who were they anyway, and what did they want? Dad and Ollie told terrible stories about some of the things they had done to others who had come by in covered wagons. I couldn't imagine what we would do if we met up with any of that kind.

We walked quite a ways until we indeed found a wide path, and we followed it an even longer way until it came to the creek. Then we followed the creek and, sure enough, there on the side of a big hill were the springs gushing out the side of it. It was not as noisy as Ollie had told us it would be, but rather a pleasant, bubbly sound. It made Edythe and me have to squat and potty before we could reach our pails in and catch some of the fresh, clear, bubbling water.

No one was there that evening, but it was almost dark so we didn't stay long. We drank our bellies full of that fresh, cold water, filled our pails, and started back, remembering forever how that water tasted. We had heard the story that this water had something special in it that would make you well if you were sick. We thought that if only Ollie would drink the whole pail just once she would get the color back in her face again. The folks seemed happy when we got back that night and drank most the water we had brought and put the rest of it into the water can. Dad and Ollie asked us a thousand questions about the path and the springs and then finally told us to go back one more time. Only this time, when we got our pails full, we were supposed to look for Indians. But what was the point? It was too dark to see anything by then.

We were even more scared walking in the dark, and we tried to hold hands on one side and swing the pails on the other. We found that it was too hard to walk together that way so we stopped. We figured out that we had to walk with opposite feet if we were going to hold hands.

The challenge was to walk with pails of water without spilling them. We laughed and giggled until we got everything just right as we walked in the moonlight. We lost a lot of water along the way, and we both got a big swat on the butt from Dad when we got back before he sent us into the wagon for the rest of the night.

The next morning the can was full. Ollie and Dad had made many sneak visits back to the spring that night. We left soon after that because Ollie was so skittish about the Indians. I had hoped that we could stay longer so the water would have a chance to make Ollie feel stronger. Right then I decided that someday I would come back and drink more of that special water!

As we made our way into Minnesota, Dad seemed to relax, and we traveled a little slower. He even let the horses walk at their normal speed, meandering along at their own leisurely pace. The folks let us walk alongside to pick dandelions in the warm sunshine, but the days seemed extra long when it rained. When the wagon got wet, it would stink from the creosote. Our legs got cramped from sitting so long, and, of course, there was always a tiff or two between us kids that sent one of us crying or sniffling. We knew we'd be in trouble with Dad if we fussed too long or loud so we always tried to quiet each other down before Dad reached back to settle the dispute with his own rough hand across the head or face of the closest kid. We always knew when it was time for him to sneak into a town for a night of drinking because he got mean and nasty a few days before. Sometimes I wished he would go to town and never come back because there was always a squabble or fight when he did. I felt so sorry for Ollie taking those beatings all the time.

In spite of everything, we settled down into some sort of routine as we traveled--always hunting for water or trying to find some kind of wildlife to snag for supper. Sometimes Dad took a chance and went up someone's driveway or field when they were outside and asked for water. And once in a while he came back with some fixings for a meal as well as clean water. What a feast we had! Ollie proclaimed on those occasions, "We're eating like kings!" At least we went to bed with full tummies.

Some nights Ollie put our blankets under the wagon, and we went to sleep outside watching the moon come up. Edythe and I argued about whose friend the moon was. I noticed that the moon followed me when I walked, and when I stopped the moon stopped. So I decided the moon was my friend. But Edythe noticed the same thing when she walked, so she decided the moon was her friend. There were many arguments between us, especially when the moon was out.

It took many weeks, almost all summer, to get where we were going. We were thrilled when the folks told us that we were not very far from Brainerd. Dad said the air smelled different up there. We didn't know what he meant by that; we couldn't smell any difference in the air. We did find more places to fish than we had before. Ollie always got excited when we came around a curve and saw a lake or a deep river. She made us fishing poles out of tree branches and used some of her butcher string for lines so we could try our hand at fishing. She was talented at figuring out how to do things. Sometimes we waded in the water, often getting in too far so our clothes got all wet. Ollie used that for an excuse to get out the soap to wash our clothes. Then we ran around in our birthday suits, as Ollie liked to call them, swimming in the creeks, often coming out with leeches clinging to our bodies. Ollie had to pick them off. Yuck! But we always ate well when we had fish. Ollie even saw to it that we had potatoes once in a while. Usually they were very small and scrubby, but she said that was better than nothing at all.

We all thrived in the warm summer sun. Edythe and I got such tans when we walked all day. Ollie said we looked just like little Indians with our dark skins. I didn't know if that was good or bad. I had never seen an Indian, but I had sure heard enough about them along the way.

As we got closer to Brainerd, Dad and Ollie warned us to stay close to the wagon when we tried to roam and explore in the evenings. They never let us play hide-and-seek in the bushes. We always had to stay near the fire and go to bed extra early. Ollie said there might be Indians lurking around. She said they would sneak up and steal us away to their village of tents, where we would be raised as Indians. We were so scared that we started crying when she told us those stories. Ollie also loved to tell stories about when she was a little kid. These stories were fun and didn't scare us. And she sang songs, one after another. She tried to teach us some of them, and we did our best to sing along as much as we could.

The only thing bad about the whole trip was the MOSQUITOES! They were just terrible — biting all the time. We tried to outrun them, but they could fly just as fast as we could run. Poor Billy, he got the worst of them. Ollie liked to say, "They seem to make a meal off him every chance they get." Violet was too little to know enough to swat mosquitoes, but she got pretty good at it by the time we arrived in Brainerd.

Dad said that it would be just another week or two before we got to Grandpa and Grandma Green's cabin. Grandma Green was my dad's mother, and Grandpa Green was his stepfather. We had never seen our grandparents, but Dad said they would let us move in with them. Wow! They must be awfully nice people to do that for a big bunch like us! We could hardly wait. Just think . . . no stinky wagon, no more cramped legs, no more running to catch up with the wagon when we got too far behind. We could sleep in a bed again, away from the mosquitoes at last!

Ollie said there would even be time for her to concoct some of that delicious soup she used to make when we were back living in our cabin. That seemed terribly long ago. I wondered if our dog was still waiting for us to come back, and would Mommy be sitting on the steps wondering where we went? How would she ever find us again? I often started crying when I thought about these things.

When we finally arrived in the Brainerd area, we stayed for a few days. I remember Ollie saying she wanted to visit some people to see if we could get help with food and other things. She also said something about washing up and going to see the preacher. We were told to stay behind. She said that Edythe and I should be old enough to take care of Billy and Violet. We should remember to keep them in sight and not let them cry. Dad went along with her, but he was angry! He wasn't going to "see no preacher," he said. He told her that he was going to wait for her at the pub. We realized by now that he meant the "whiskey place."

We did have fun playing that day. We played hide-and-seek in the woods. Billy sat and counted for us while we hid, and then one of us had to find the others. Even Violet was getting good at finding us under a bush or behind some trees or logs. Ollie had left us some flat bread to eat, and said she was going to bring back molasses if we were good.

She came back late that day. I don't remember when Dad came back, but I guess it was even later. He told Ollie the next day that he was looking for some kind of job. But he was awfully crabby again! Ollie said it was from the whiskey he drank. At least Ollie had brought the molasses. She also brought back flour, dried peas, beans, and of course our beloved crackers. She even remembered a big bar of wash soap. We sure had fun that evening washing ourselves in the creek with that soap and the bubbles it made. *Sally remembered that day every time she took a wrapper off a new bar of soap.*

Dad and Ollie talked a lot to us kids the next few days as we started on the road again. They said that we would soon be coming to Grandma and Grandpa Green's cabin. They mentioned that it was close to a place called Merrifield. I wondered how many people lived there. Was it like Clear Lake where I was born, or would it be as big as Davenport, the town where we had come from?

The only important thing we had to remember was that Grandma was very sick. Dad told us that she had arthritis. He explained that arthritis makes the bones and body extremely stiff. Grandma had to spend the whole day in a wheelchair that Grandpa Green had built for her. Billy was happy to hear that. He said that at last someone would stay sitting long enough to visit him when he was tired. We all laughed at him.

The excitement at finally being somewhere had put everyone in a good mood. We kids were tired of traveling and moving every day. Just think, we were going to have a field all our own to roll in and make rooms in the tall grass for our playhouses. We wouldn't have to make new ones all the time. We could just stay in one place and play!

We told Dad to get a cow right away so we could have milk every day. Ollie even thought that was a good idea. Edythe and I were so happy that we rolled and laughed and wrecked everything in the wagon fooling around. Ollie got really angry with us then, and we had to straighten everything up.

## *Chapter 6*
## *The End of a Journey*

Those last few days of travel before we got to Grandpa and Grandma Green's cabin took forever. Maybe it was because we were so excited to see the "old folks" (that's what Ollie called them). But Dad said we were taking it slow because the horses' feet were sore from walking so long without shoes. Edythe and I talked about that. We said we'd have sore feet, too, if we had to walk all the way from Iowa without any shoes. We actually didn't have any shoes, but we could ride in the wagon when we wanted to rest.

We came upon Grandpa and Grandma's cabin late in the afternoon. Grandpa was out working in the garden, and Grandma was sitting in her wheelchair on the porch watching him. I don't remember who was the most excited when we saw each other—them or us! Edythe and I jumped off the wagon and ran the rest of the way. We hugged and kissed and almost made Grandma fall out of her chair. Everyone was so happy. We were at the end of our journey at last. And just think—a cabin to spend the night in! Grandpa made extra that night for supper, and we ate and ate until we thought our bellies would explode. Then we sat outside and watched the sun go down over by the lake. At least Grandma said there was a lake over there. We couldn't see it from the cabin, but Grandpa said he would show us the way in the morning.

Edythe and I went to gather fresh grass for Billy to sleep on, but Grandpa Green found an old blanket for him. We all felt thankful for Grandpa's generosity when we slept in the cabin that night. The kids slept on the floor, and Ollie and Dad slept in a little bed set up in the corner. Grandpa slept sitting up in his favorite chair. But after that first night, Ollie and Dad moved out to the covered wagon and let Grandpa have his little bed back.

Grandma's big bed took up all the room in their bedroom. She was so crippled that when Grandpa laid her down, she stayed in the same sitting position as when she had been in the wheelchair. We all giggled when Grandpa put the blankets over her legs. They were still bent, and it looked like there was a room under the sheets. Grandma just couldn't straighten out at all. We felt sorry for her but couldn't keep from laughing when it was time for bed. She even laughed when she saw us kids laughing and pretty soon, everyone was laughing!

We loved staying at the cabin because we were in one place and didn't have to leave. Even the horses seemed to enjoy grazing in the nearby pasture. Every time we looked at them, they were hanging their heads sleeping. Dad said it was because they were awfully tired from the trip. "They sure look skinny," Grandpa said. It was good that he had a big pasture where the horses could eat their hearts out and sleep whenever they wanted to.

Billy even seemed to feel a little better. Just having a place to call his own made a big difference to him. He slept a lot too. When he was able to get enough sleep, he didn't have any bad spells. The spells were awful. He thrashed around, foamed at the mouth, and sometimes bit his tongue until it bled. When he finally did quiet down, he'd sleep for a long time. When he woke up, the first thing he always asked was, "What time is it?" I hoped I could get him a watch of his own someday. When he was fully awake and his body was still, he loved to talk. He talked all the time. We couldn't shut him up. And he loved to try to sing and whistle. Ollie tried to teach us some of the songs that her grandpa had taught her. We loved it when she sang. She sounded much prettier than we did.

Dad said he was going to work on Billy one of these days to try and make him stronger. We never knew what he meant by that until later. The folks talked to Grandpa and Grandma about getting Violet to a doctor for her ears, but nothing was ever done.

We rested a long time at Grandpa's place, and we all ate well. We never went to bed hungry while we were there. We always had something fresh out of the garden, and Grandpa took us to the lake, where we fished from shore. We caught more fish than what the folks wanted to clean. They tried to show Edythe and me how to clean fish, but we didn't do very well with the knife. Grandma said she could do better, even with her sore fingers, so she got the nasty job of cleaning the fish. It was always our job to take the innards out to the garden afterward and bury them deep in the ground. Grandpa said it made the soil black for the next year.

He had a cow so we got to drink all the milk she gave. I asked Grandpa if we could milk the cow three times a day instead of two. That way we could have even more milk to drink. Grandpa just laughed his big, hearty laugh and said, "No, that wouldn't be a good idea!"

One day he took all three of us girls for a walk. We didn't have to walk far before we came to the general store on the main street of Merrifield. The candy was in the front case right near the door, so we spotted it the minute we walked in. If we were very quiet and polite when Grandpa was talking to the clerk, he would buy us some penny candy. We always remembered to bring a piece back to Billy since he was too weak to walk the path to the store. Grandpa mentioned that he was going to make Billy a wagon to ride in so he could come with us next time. Then Violet could ride too. She was little and always tagged way behind.

***Sarah with Grandpa Green's cats***

Ollie and Grandma talked often of finding us a bigger place to stay. They said that the cabin was just too small for all of us to bunk in when it got cold out. We'd be climbing the walls by spring with all those kids inside. I remember the day when Dad and Grandpa came back from a wagon ride out into the woods. Grandpa said that they had found the empty cabin that he'd heard about and tied string around a tree by the path so they could find it later. Ollie thought that we should take a peek at it ourselves. We were a little worried about living in the deep woods, but Dad said it would be good for us. "Just think," he added, "we would never have to be afraid of anyone coming to take us away again." We all hooted and hollered when he said that!

***Grandpa and Grandma Green pose with their three sons; Windsor is in the middle.***

# Chapter 7
## We Found Heaven

After finding that old, empty cabin, we were awfully busy. Every day we would ride out there and clean the place. One day Edythe swept the floor so hard with the broom that dust and dirt kicked up something terrible. I hollered at her to stop, but she wouldn't listen so I grabbed the broom away from her. She got upset and chased me all over the place trying to retrieve it. I kept running with it farther and farther away out into the woods, running so fast and so far that I finally fell to the ground, completely out of breath. Edythe caught up to me, and we rolled around in the tall grass until we were totally exhausted.

We began looking around, and as we sat down, we marveled at our surroundings. We realized we had run into a clearing among the trees. The trees were just beginning to turn pretty colors, and the birds were singing so loudly we could hardly talk to each other. We found ourselves sitting close to a pond filled with ducks and other critters. The sun was getting low in the sky, and clouds floated by ever so slowly. Edythe and I lay down in the grass and just listened to all the beautiful sounds around us. We said that maybe we had found heaven! We decided not to tell anyone about our special, secret place. We wanted to keep it to ourselves. We stayed ever so long—until the sun had nearly set–before we thought of trying to find our way back to the cabin.

We knew that Ollie was going to be upset that we had run off without telling her. We figured she would probably be hollering her head off trying to find us, and even talked about the likelihood of a paddling when we got back.

But we were afraid of the dark more than a paddling so we kept winding our way around trees and through the thicket until we could hear Ollie's voice. We headed that way and soon found our way home.

As we lay in our beds that night still hurting from our butt whippings, we talked about whether we would ever be able to find our way back to that special spot. We decided then and there that next time we went to Grandpa's cabin we would bring string and tie it around the trees to mark the path to our "heaven."

Grandpa Green took Edythe and me to the general store soon after that. There he bought rope for our beds. He had plans of tying the rope onto nails on the outside walls of the cabin and then onto boards that he had roughed out from trees. Then, during the day, the beds could be drawn up to the side of the wall. At night we could lower the rope, and the bed would drop for us to sleep on. We had enough rope for three beds—Edythe's, Violet's, and mine. We knew that Billy would have to sleep on the floor so he wouldn't get hurt when he had his spells. Grandpa showed us how to fill our mattresses that he and Grandma had made from mattress ticking with grass and leaves.

It was fun watching our cabin turn from a dirty mess into a nice home. Ollie and Grandma made curtains for the windows out of gunny sacks. They put nails into each side of the window frame, threaded heavy butcher string through the top of each curtain hem, and attached the string to the nails. They looked beautiful. "Besides," Ollie said, "the Indians won't be able to look in our windows now."

That was our first reminder that we weren't the only ones living in those woods. At first we were scared and didn't want to stay in the cabin when the folks weren't there because we wouldn't know what to do. Ollie said that we should just run away as fast as we could and try to hide in the woods. Then the Indians wouldn't take us. We wondered for a long time about what Ollie said. The Indians would take us where? Back to Iowa or to their city of tents? God forbid! Edythe and I sat up many nights talking about what we would do with Billy and Violet if that ever happened. We finally decided that we would shove Billy under our beds to hide him after we let them down from the wall. We also decided to take turns carrying Violet while we ran out into the wilderness. Such thoughts for such little ones!

We started staying out in the cabin more and more often now that it had been made livable. Since there was no indoor stove yet, we had to fix our meals out on the open fire pit that Dad had dug in the clearing. Grandpa and Dad worked very hard to clear the trees out, and it was really starting to look nice. We even asked Grandpa if he had any more rope left to make us a swing. There was a big branch hanging from a tree nearby that would make a perfect place to hang a swing. Grandpa just smiled as he stopped from his work and wiped his brow. Soon after that, Grandpa came with a long piece of rope and hung us the best swing in the whole world. We swung for hours from that tree! I even worried about wearing it out by swinging on it too much. Dad mentioned that he was going to find Ollie a decent stove for cooking in the cabin as soon as he found work. He said we would need something before winter set in. We couldn't keep cooking and eating outside all winter because the snow would be too deep for us to find the fire pit.

I sure missed my mom, and I got really angry when I thought about how she just left us behind and never came back. Why would she do that? What did we do? Then I would start sniffling again.

Grandpa came out often to help Dad with the work, and we ate supper together out there near the pit. When we were all finished, Grandpa would get his fiddle out and play beautiful music. He even sang some lovely songs. All of us felt true contentment and happiness as we sat all evening listening to him. He sang the same songs over and over again, but we didn't care. Edythe and I tried memorizing them and then singing them when he wasn't there. *These were the very songs that Sally taught her children.* It was then that I remembered hearing my real mother sing. Her dad would come with his fiddle and sing like that too.

Not all of our evenings were that pleasant though. There were many nights when Grandpa wouldn't come, and Ollie and Dad would sit and drink their bootleg whiskey, as they liked to call it. They really got out of sorts and crabby when we kids were around and often chased us off into the woods for long periods of time. Sometimes we bedded down and slept out in the woods all night, not coming home until morning. Poor Billy! He always had to stay behind and take the beatings from Dad and his liquor temper.

I remember Dad commenting one evening that Billy would get better if he only exercised more, so he started making him walk around the clearing of the cabin. Around and around they went. This routine often lasted far into the night. If Billy fell to the ground from exhaustion, Dad would beat on his back. Sometimes he would use his belt, sometimes his hands, and sometimes a piece of log or board. When Billy fell from the beatings, Dad made him crawl on his hands and knees around the clearing. Sometimes Dad came in and went to bed, seeming to sleep. Billy was supposed to keep walking or crawling around the clearing. But when Billy stopped to catch his breath or fell again, Dad only yelled louder, threatening to beat him even more if he had to come out!

The more Dad drank, the more he picked on Billy. In his extreme state of drunkenness, he decided that Billy should run instead of walk. So he got the belt out and kept beating on Billy until he passed out or had another fit. Then Dad would leave him alone out there in the clearing while the rest of us had to go inside to bed. Poor Billy! I felt so sorry for him, but when I tried to go out and help him, Dad would take the belt to me too! We soon learned not to go near Billy or Dad when Dad was in that kind of a mood!

One time Dad beat Billy so badly with a log that his head was split wide open, and he bled and was unconscious for many days. I sneaked out after dark to try to cover him with something and wake him and give him a drink. After that, Billy got so weak that he couldn't even come out of the cabin to sit with us by the fire. We would take supper to him while he lay in the corner on his bed of leaves and swamp grass. It took forever to heal his head. He had an indentation on the back side of his head for the rest of his life, big enough for me to lay my finger in. After that, he either just slept or had those terrible spells. When he was awake, he was so weak he could hardly whisper. He often asked me for the time. We never had any kind of time keeper in the cabin so I made up a time of day just to keep him happy.

## *Chapter 8*
## *Time for School*

Not long after we settled into our cabin, Grandpa Green came by to tell us that we had to go to school. We had worn out the one dress we were given at the orphanage in Iowa and longed for a new one. But Dad said there was no money for such things. I remember Ollie and Grandma talking about it one day when we went to visit Grandma and Grandpa Green at their cabin. When we would make the trip to visit Grandma and Grandpa, we would take the wagon that Grandpa had made us and sit Billy in it. Edythe and I took turns pulling him. Ollie never helped much because of her crippled leg. Sometimes Violet would sit in it, too, but that made the wagon hard to pull along the path. We didn't go often, but when we did it was really something special.

To help us find our way, we tied ribbons along the path from the clearing of our cabin out to the railroad tracks. Then we turned right and followed the tracks about two miles. After that we watched for the ribbons that told us to turn into the woods that led to Grandpa's place.

On one of our visits, Ollie and Grandma decided to hunt through Grandma Green's old trunks and Mother's trunk for material. They must have found something because they made Edythe and me lie on the floor, on top of the fabric, and they cut around us to make the right size dress. My dress had blue flowers, and Edythe got the one with yellow flowers. Little Violet cried because she didn't get a new one, but Grandma let it be known that she would find more material and make Violet her own special dress. "Besides, she is too little to go to school," Grandma said. "And, of course, she's deaf so she couldn't learn anyway!"

Billy just stayed outside sitting in the wagon quietly, and I wondered what he was thinking when he heard us talking about going to school and getting new clothes. I hated to think of him being sad because he wasn't included.

The next time we went to visit Grandma Green, she had two new pairs of underpants waiting for Edythe and me. She had cut them out of her dish towel material and stitched them by hand while in her wheelchair. We didn't think anything could top that, but Grandpa Green took us to the general store in town that same day and bought us each a new pair of brown shoes! We danced all the way back to the cabin, which was about two miles south of Merrifield.

*Sarah and Edythe, ready for school near Merrifield, 1921*

Finally we were ready for our first day at school. When the big day came, Grandpa came to get us in his wagon, and away we went through the woods and down the road about three miles to the school. After that first day he showed us how to take a shortcut through the woods so the trip wouldn't be as long. It was a long hike, but as youngsters we didn't mind because we were always so busy talking about the day's events. Besides, if we were late getting home, Ollie always tried to finish most of our chores for us.

Edythe wanted to take the long, easy path. That way Ollie was sure to have her chores done. She hated her job of gathering wood for the fire. Mine was to clean up the mess in Billy's bed, give him fresh bedding, and clean him up for the day. I never had time to do it in the morning because we always had to get going much too early.

School started at 9 a.m., and the teacher started classes on time whether we were there or not. If we were late, we had to stay after school for as long as we were late in the morning. If we were too late, we got a whipping from the teacher. Then school wasn't so much fun. I begged Dad to get us a clock like Grandpa had so we could at least start off to get to school on time.

Edythe and I were put in the same class because we were so close in age. We were the only ones in school that year in that grade. There would be no school for Billy. He wasn't able to make the trip to school or sit up long enough to learn. Grandpa didn't even tell the school about Billy when we went to register, but we would come home every day and tell him everything we had learned.

I remember the teacher gave us each a tablet and pencil. We were so proud. I took my pencil and paper home most every day so I could write and draw for Billy. He was always excited and interested to hear about our day and hardly gave us time to change out of our school clothes before he started begging for us to tell all. Billy actually was a help to us because he drilled Edythe and me on our new spelling words and arithmetic figures. Billy's mind was much more alert than anyone gave him credit for as he seemed to learn faster than we did. He would even write up arithmetic problems for us to figure out and then correct them. In between fits, Billy would lie in his bed and write the letters of the alphabet for hours on end the way we had showed him. He practiced numbers too, and before long he was figuring out his own arithmetic problems. Then he would sleep for a while and start all over again. Billy was a wonderful brother, and Edythe and I loved him so.

We attended classes until Christmas, when school recessed through the deep of the winter. We ended that school session with a Christmas party or program that all the folks came to watch. Afterward we ate a meal together before we headed home for the long winter vacation. I remember that first winter when we said good-bye to our newfound schoolmates whom we wouldn't see again until late March. The spring session lasted all the way until the end of June.

Tragically, there was a family with two girls and one boy who left in their wagon that cold December evening after the Christmas party, never to be heard from again. The wagon was found in the early spring by someone walking in the woods. It had been destroyed, and all of their belongings had been ransacked or were missing. The horses were gone, and the members of the family beaten and left for dead. The story going around was that renegade Indians had slaughtered the family and taken their horses. Once again I was frightened by a tale about Indians who wanted to harm us. Who were they anyway? What did they look like? Why would they do such terrible things?

## *Chapter 9*
## *To Add to Our Misery*

That winter seemed cold and long, partly because we didn't have enough warm clothing to go outside. Dad very seldom found work, and when he did it was just for the day. When we started school again in March, we walked to school every morning, shivering and wearing only a sweater and a light coat that Edythe and I had to share. She got cold and shivered first when she wore the sweater and I the coat. Then we would exchange wraps. When I would start to shiver, we would trade once again. When it was raining, we would run as fast as we could, figuring that somehow we could outrun the rain.

We often found shelter under some bush and shared the sweater, wrapped up together until the rain slowed enough for us to continue. Then there was always the problem of our new shoes getting wet. When they did get wet, we took them off and dried them on the oven door, but they ended up crooked. They didn't fit the next day when we tried to put them on. If only we could have gone to school without shoes! But the rule was, "No shoes—no school."

Our nights inside the cabin were also long and hard. We never had enough kerosene to light the lamp for the whole evening. We would use it only long enough to eat and do our schoolwork. Then Ollie would blow it out, and we would sit around talking in the dark or go to bed and talk there just to stay warm. We seemed to be always short on wood for the stove too.

To add to our misery, Dad never made it home in the evenings after helping Grandpa Green cut wood and working for the lumber mill without being "all tanked out of shape," as Ollie put it. Then the beatings started. He would beat her so bad! When the pain got too unbearable, she ran out of the cabin into the cold night, and we often didn't see her again until morning, after Dad left. When this happened, we were left alone with this frightening, mean old man. To keep us from running off like Ollie did, he came around and tied our arms to the bed with a rope. Sometimes he took either Edythe or me into his bed and did naughty things to us. We were threatened, spanked, or beaten until we played his "peter games" with him. If we refused, we were batted about on our heads and beaten to the floor until we submitted to whatever he asked us to do.

It kept getting worse as time went on, and we would often be put back into our beds bleeding and crying. We were so scared of him, but we saw no way out. Often he would tie Ollie to her bed so she couldn't help us. If she tried, he would beat her something terrible, and she would lie in bed for days, unable to move. She tried so hard to make things better, but nothing seemed to change with Dad. It had to be his way or else. I often wonder what the teacher thought of us coming to school looking so bad after these terrible nights.

We were ecstatic when spring came because we could run away outside when Dad got into one those moods. Ollie couldn't run very far or fast because she was so crippled. She suffered terribly that first year.

## *Chapter 10*
## *The Old Blue Sweater*

That spring Dad talked of getting a big job. He had heard of the farmers out in North and South Dakota hiring men to come to help with the wheat and grain when it was ready to harvest. He also heard that he could ride the trains out there and work until the harvest was finished and come home in the fall before Christmas with lots of money in his pocket. One of the best parts was that we wouldn't have to put up with Dad and his whisky temper all the time. I don't remember just when he left, but it was around the end of the school year. Since Dad was already gone, we got Grandpa and Grandma Green to come to our school picnic, and they picked us up in their wagon. What a wonderful day! Grandpa even brought his fiddle and played for the teacher and kids. We felt so proud to be able to show off our grandparents.

That was a happy time in our lives. We seemed to thrive in the summer sun. Grandpa brought Ollie seeds to plant in a garden spot that he had dug for us along with special planting potatoes that we couldn't eat. "They're just for planting," he said. We often got water from the creek to clean our cabin, and we teased Ollie, telling her she was a cleaning fool. She was always cleaning when we wanted to play. But she insisted we stay around and help her every day to keep things looking nice. Another chore was listening for the cowbell. When we heard it nearby, our job was to run out and milk the cow and bring back what we could to the cabin. Fresh milk was a special treat. Out came the crackers, and we ate crackers and milk until our tummies seemed about to burst. Springtime also brought fresh asparagus and rhubarb, which we delighted in hunting down.

The natural treats kept coming as the warm days set in. Edythe and I, and sometimes Violet, looked for berries in the woods. We seemed to know just where blueberries and raspberries grew. Blackberries and boysenberries were also around if we looked hard enough. Ollie had a special way to snare rabbits so we often feasted on them. She was good at snaring squirrels too. We saw many deer, but Ollie never had the gun or the guts to shoot one. She thought they were too smart and pretty.

As summer moved closer to fall, Ollie got quieter and more depressed when we talked about Dad coming home. She sat on the porch and cried for hours sometimes. We knew we had lots of money coming home with Dad, but we were all troubled about spending another winter caught in the cabin with him. Even Billy got stronger and braver with Dad gone. He tried hard to go out and cut wood or clean up the clearing the best he could. He loved to whistle, and I remember him whistling all that summer, even when he was inside. Often he would whistle us a tune he had made up. He told us he didn't know how to fiddle (as far as that goes, we didn't even own a fiddle), but he could whistle tunes. We heard some beautiful songs coming out of Billy that summer.

By the time school started again, we were all healthy and "brown as Indians," Ollie said. We had to ask Grandpa Green for new shoes as well as another coat, so Ollie took us down the path, hauling Billy and Violet in the wagon. We followed the tracks into Merrifield and turned at the familiar colored ribbon Grandpa had tied to the trees. That was where we turned to get to their cabin. Billy was strong enough that summer to walk a ways. Once in a while he had a spell so we stopped, sat down and waited for him to finish his sleep that followed the seizure. Then we continued on our way.

Ollie got what we needed at the general store and charged it to Dad's account until he returned with all that money to pay the bill. The store clerk seemed to understand. He never argued with Ollie over our bill. I remember Ollie buying thread for our new dresses but not material. Grandma Green had more in her trunk. We always picked up white soda crackers for our crackers and milk.

We trotted off to school happy as larks that fall while Billy and Violet stayed behind crying on the porch. We felt so sorry for Billy not being able to go to school. He was smart but sick too often so it just wouldn't work. We promised to bring our learning home to him just like what we had done the year before.

One day I will always remember it was raining hard and getting colder by the minute. We waited to start out for school, thinking the rain would let up, but it never did. Ollie had been up all night crying quietly in her room, and I had gone in to see her a couple of times to ask if she was sick or something. She just hugged me and told me she would always love me but that I should go back to bed. That next morning, while it was raining so hard, she packed us a lunch of homemade biscuits and lard sandwiches. She even put in a couple of crackers, and we teased her about not having a way to carry milk to eat with them. She just laughed through her tears and hugged us once more and told us to get going even if it was raining as we needed to go to school and not to forget to share our only sweater.

Wow, was that sweater ever getting worn out! It had a hole in the sleeve because we'd had a squabble earlier. Edythe had torn it on a bush while running away from me. Ollie said she would try to figure out a way for us to start wearing our coats the next day if it was still so cold. We left late that morning running down our little path that was a shortcut through the woods. Ollie stayed back on the porch with Billy and Violet, waving and calling that she loved us until we were out of hearing distance. When I look back on it now, that was very unusual behavior for her.

The rain continued all that day so we were all wet and soaked to the skin when we got home from school. Ollie was nowhere to be found. We asked Billy if he knew where Ollie could be. He told us that she had packed a bag with her clothes and was going to town. She didn't say if it was Merrifield or Brainerd. She also told him that he was big enough now to take care of Violet. He figured that maybe it would be Brainerd as long as she took clothes. He had asked to go along, but she said it was raining too hard to take Violet out, and that he should take care of her until she got back. Billy said she hugged them both and told them she loved them and left crying. He thought that since she hadn't come back by the time we got home from school she had gone to Brainerd to talk to the preacher like she had done when we first came up here.

We weren't too worried about it that night. We hadn't heard the usual cowbells that evening and figured it was raining too hard for any critters to be out and about. We fixed a supper of warm mush without milk, did our homework, and went to bed, where we discovered that Ollie had left our coats folded up between our blanket and mattress. Billy got up that night to put wood in the stove for the first time in his life, and the next morning Edythe and I dressed, hauled in wood for Billy and Violet to have for the day, put on our coats for the first time, and went on our way to school.

# Chapter 11
## Gimpy, the Dog

We spent the rest of the week doing just what Ollie would have wanted us to do. We did our chores after school, made our mush, did our homework, put the lamp out early, and talked of what would happen when Dad got home with all his money. We kept hoping to see Ollie walk through the door any time. One night we got really brave and opened up a jar of Ollie's homemade applesauce to eat with our crackers.

When Ollie didn't return by the weekend, Edythe and I really started to worry. We figured maybe she got sick running out in the rain that day without a coat. We decided to just wait and see. We honestly felt she would come back soon so we kept up with our normal routine. We were getting pretty courageous by this time. After all, I was nearly 10 and Edythe nearly 9, Billy was 7, and Violet was 5 years old.

When Saturday came and there was still no Ollie, we decided to walk over to Grandpa Green's cabin to tell him. We took the wagon with Violet and Billy and spent the day. They were just as surprised to hear that Ollie had left as we were. Grandpa agreed that maybe she had gotten sick in town and would heal before she came back.

We were very surprised to see that Grandpa had gotten a dog since we had seen him last. He said it had come into the camp while he was out cutting lumber. The dog was a beautiful brown color, but only had three legs. Grandpa said that it looked like he had gotten his leg caught in a trap that pulled it off. The leg had healed fairly well, but Grandpa put some tar on it to keep the bugs off until the flesh wasn't exposed anymore. He said that we could take the dog home with us. We were all so excited! We were going to have a new dog to replace Pepper. Grandpa told us to give him some of our leftovers every night after supper so Gimpy would stay with us on the porch to watch over us until Ollie got back. He told us the dog would bark whenever anyone got too close to the cabin. If that were to happen, we should latch the door and put a chair under the doorknob so they couldn't get in. We were so happy to walk home that night with our own dog on a rope following along behind the wagon. Grandpa thought we should call him Gimpy because he gimped along so funny with just three legs.

Billy stayed in the cabin every day with Violet and Gimpy to try to keep them busy while Edythe and I went to school. He told us it was the hardest thing he had ever done because Violet was always hungry, and there wasn't a lot to fix without Ollie there. One day he heard the cowbell so he went out to see which direction it was coming from, but he was too weak to go after it. Violet was by his side so he motioned the way for her to go, and she trotted off into the pasture with her little syrup pail and Gimpy running along beside her. She had been with Edythe and me to milk often enough that she seemed to know just what to do. At least Billy thought so.

He waited much too long for her and the dog to come back. When they didn't return, he started down the trail himself. He didn't have to go far before he heard her hollering and screaming. The dog was making a fuss too. Billy was slow and frail, but he kept going ever so slowly until he came upon her struggling in a mud hole near the slough where the cows were grazing. Violet had tried to go directly to the cows when she got bogged down with muck and had wrestled her way deeper and deeper into a hole in the ground. He tried to pull her out, but between the dog pulling on her dress and Billy tugging on her arm, she just kept squealing louder and louder and sinking deeper and deeper. He finally gave up and sat with her to quiet her until we got home.

We were surprised when Gimpy met us on the path near the cabin. Billy had always kept him inside during the day. We knew something was wrong so we started to run. There was no one home or on the porch, but we knew just which way to look because Gimpy kept running up and down the trail to the pasture. We found Billy and Violet both sobbing and sitting in the mud hole. Violet looked just terrible! Her dress was torn to bits, and she was covered in mud from her head to her toes. Billy didn't look much better. All three of us tugged and pulled until the muck finally gave up its prize little girl to some very dedicated siblings.

With Violet finally free and sitting safely on our laps, we hugged and cried quite freely for some time. Even Gimpy was full of mud but wiggled and bounced with excitement. It took us the rest of the night to get ourselves back to the cabin and get cleaned up. We even tried to give Gimpy a bath with the rest of the water we had left after taking baths and washing our school clothes. This was all done in a washtub in front of the stove. We fell into bed totally exhausted when we were finished, wet and cold from the unheated water we had to use from the creek.

Edythe and I overslept and didn't make it to school the next day. Anyway, our clothes still weren't dry from our little episode the night before. Another week had gone by, and still no Ollie.

## Chapter 12
## The Empty Window

Edythe and I talked often after that day about the possibility of Violet getting into trouble again. We were worried about Billy being alone with her all day so we decided we should take turns going to school. That way Billy and Violet wouldn't have to be left alone. We both agreed that Billy wasn't strong enough to tend to Violet all day every day.

We decided not to tell anyone but Grandpa Green about our being home alone. We knew that Dad would be home soon, and we didn't want any trouble with the school board or anyone else. We came up with the idea that we would both take turns being "sick" a couple of days a week. That way no one would have to know. I remember Edythe and me lying in our beds talking way into the night about our situation. Billy would often call to us to "shut up and go to sleep!" But we were too concerned to sleep. Edythe would try to make fun of the situation. She would say crazy things like she was going to try to get a boyfriend so he could come home with us. Then he could bring the wood in instead of her having to do it all the time. He could even carry the water from the creek too. She was always trying to get out of work. I told her that Grandpa Green would help us if we really needed him.

We were so destitute for food that we took the wagon to Merrifield the next weekend. We had decided not to mention to anyone at the store that we were alone at home and had all hugged and promised each other that we would keep this pact no matter what.

We picked up a big flour sack of crackers and a new bar of soap. We were still lucky to have potatoes from the garden as well as some jars of vegetables that Ollie had canned. We rationed out the vegetables— one jar a week. We ate potatoes two times a week and decided to try fishing when it was warm enough. The lake was a little ways away, but we would try. We also picked up a big can of lard and a sack of flour. The fellow at the general store asked us why we came alone. We told him that Dad was still out west and Ollie was "ailing" so she sent us. He just smiled and said nothing. He even gave us a sack of penny candy when we left. What a treat! We promised him that Dad would come to pay the bill when he got home.

We made our way back that day skipping and laughing as we went down the railroad bed thinking how smart we were to fool everyone. Billy and Violet could hardly wait until we got home to eat that candy. We went to bed that night full of crackers and milk and hard candy. We really thought we had the world by the tail. We had all our problems figured out. If only it weren't so cold outside.

We kept up this kind of a routine until Christmas vacation came. Either Edythe or I would attend school on any given day. Sometimes I couldn't get that lazy Edythe out of bed to get to school, but I always tried to go when it was my day. Grandpa came out to check on us whenever he had the time. He helped us cut wood and stacked it next to the cabin. He brought groceries for us when he could.

We began to worry about Violet and her dress. It was so ragged after the mud incident. We talked long and hard about how we could get her another one without going to Grandpa. We decided the only thing to do was to take the curtains down from the windows and use them to make her a new dress. We wondered if we would have trouble with the Indians looking in, but we hadn't had any trouble with them yet so we figured we would be okay.

**Edythe and Sarah at Grandpa Green's Cabin, 1921**

We took the curtains down and washed them one Saturday night when we finished with our baths and hung them on the line behind the stove in the kitchen to dry. This was the way we washed all our school clothes on the weekends so they got dry before we had to put them on for Monday school. Ollie had shown us that much earlier, and we were thankful. We laid Violet on the floor just the same way that Ollie and Grandma had laid Edythe and me. I felt so proud of myself when we got done sewing that dress together by hand with our big stitches. Even Violet was thrilled with a new dress. She danced round and round to whatever special music went on in a little deaf girl's head. We all watched, clapping our hands while we laughed at her dancing. We never even noticed the empty windows.

Ollie had even shown me how she made biscuits so I tried my hand at them. But when the baking powder was gone, we were in trouble until we went to the store again. We had some honey left from the time Ollie had seen a man walking along the tracks selling it. She had taken her last nickel and had gotten us a big jar. She told us we should only use it for something special. Now that she was gone, Edythe decided this must be that special time. That night we had crackers and honey with our milk. Our lard can was getting empty so the next time we went to the general store we would have to remember that too.

We were glad when Christmas came because there would be a party at school. We decided to tell Grandpa, and he went with us. When he came to pick us up in the wagon that day, he mentioned that he was going to have to decide something about us kids staying alone for the winter. I kept reassuring him that we were making out just fine and not to worry. Besides, Dad would be home any day now.

We didn't see Grandpa or Grandma for a month or so. Grandpa came to visit one day well into the winter to see how we were getting along. He said he was out in the woods looking at a new place to start cutting lumber come spring. He seemed very disturbed. He just couldn't figure out what had happened to Dad. *The records show that Windsor Richards was incarcerated in Stillwater State Prison during this time serving a seven-year sentence.* We really talked hard to convince Grandpa that we were doing just fine. He saw that we had flour and potatoes left and even counted Ollie's jars on the shelf to make sure we were being truthful. He kissed and hugged us for a long time when he left that day. We were so proud of ourselves for convincing Grandpa we were doing okay. We felt we were doing fine taking care of ourselves.

When the spring session of school started, we missed the first week without realizing it. The truant officer came one evening, but Gimpy started barking so furiously that we covered Billy with blankets, grabbed Violet, and ran into the woods. He missed us that time but sent Grandpa a letter telling him to give our folks the message that school was on for spring session, and we must report without delay. Grandpa was quite upset when he came to tell us, but we kept telling him not to worry. We would be all right until our folks got back—really we would! He said he would have to do something soon if things didn't change. We wondered what that meant. He left that day without saying good-bye.

Somehow we managed to finish out the school year without any more big problems. The teacher kept questioning us about our situation, but I guess Edythe and I made up some pretty darn good stories about missing school because she never bothered us again that spring.

**The two sisters**

## *Chapter 13*
## *The Carrot Seeds*

School ended that spring, and Edythe and I both passed into the next grade. It was good not to have to worry about who was going to school that day, and with warm weather, food was easier to find. We already knew where the asparagus patch was as well as the rhubarb. Grandpa brought us seeds for our garden and spent the day helping us dig up the ground and raking it ever so even. Then we could figure out where we wanted the rows. But he had to get back before dark so we had to do the planting without him.

Boy, we argued about where to put which packet of seeds. Billy thought one way, Edythe another, and, of course, I had my own ideas. Edythe even ran away with the carrot seed package because she wanted to plant them herself, and we all disagreed about where they should go. She hid them under a bush, but when she went back a week later they had gotten too wet to handle, much less plant. We had to go without carrots that year. We argued about those carrot seeds all our lives, and as the years went by, the story kept changing on whose fault it was that there were no carrots.

*David W. Green (Grandpa Green)*

That summer we spent our days mostly outside. We either worked at chores or playing with each other and swinging on the swing. We also tried to snare rabbits or squirrels, but we weren't very good at that. One of our favorite things to do involved packing something to eat in our syrup pails before going to our secret hiding place that we called "Heaven." We spent all day swimming naked in the pond, playing hide-and-seek, or doing whatever kids do on a summer day. Billy soaked up the sun and counted for us as we hid. It was always nearly dark when we started back. Grandpa checked up on us once a month or so, but even he seemed content to leave us alone. He did mention once or twice that something would have to be done before another winter set in.

We only had one episode that I can remember that nearly scared us to death that summer. It happened when we were getting supper ready one evening. We had played outside until dark as usual and had come in to eat before going to bed. Violet was playing on the floor when she let out a terrible howl and pointed to the window. Billy glanced up just in time to see the heads of two Indians with huge eyes peeking into the uncovered window.

For whatever reason, we didn't hear Gimpy bark. Maybe we were making too much noise just being kids trying to fix our crackers and milk and playing all at the same time. Anyway, we didn't waste any time shoving a chair against the doorknob. We sat in the dark the rest of the evening eating our meager meal while waiting for the Indians to burn the place down or something, but nothing more ever happened that night. About a week or so later we woke up to find that Gimpy wasn't on the porch. He usually slept there on hot summer nights. We went out looking for him, only to find him strung up by his one remaining hind leg in a nearby tree—dead! The Indians had gutted him and probably were planning to return soon to get the meat.

We were devastated and dropped to the ground just bawling. We stared at that carcass hanging in the tree for a very long time. We were really afraid of what the Indians would do next. For the very first time we were desperately afraid of staying alone. There was no dog to protect us anymore, and now the Indians had a face we could relate to. We slept with the chair under the doorknob every night after that and had nightmares for a long time.

We missed the start of the school year again. Only this time the school board didn't send a letter to Grandpa. They sent the truant officer out one evening to check on us in the cabin. It was beginning to get dark, and we were getting ready for bed when he broke the door down. He had sure done a good job of sneaking up on us now that we didn't have Gimpy. We scrambled into the corner behind the stove or under the beds that hung from the wall.

Everything was confusion and screaming. Poor Violet was the worst—not knowing what was happening, and I will never forget the look on Billy's face as he helplessly lay wetting his bed. We were loaded up rather quickly into a buck wagon, all of us huddled under one horse blanket as we were taken away. We were taken into a town and put into a jail cell, afraid and alone. We knew that Grandpa Green would never find us here. Where was our dad? How would Ollie find us even if she ever did come back to the cabin? We didn't even know where we were! They said we were in Little Falls when we asked, but where the heck was Little Falls anyway?

## *Chapter 14*
## *Little Falls and the Train*

It didn't take long for the city folks to hear about the four kids boarding out in the jailhouse. At first they came just to snoop and to peek in the windows. They looked at us as if we were some kind of caged animals. It was worse than seeing those Indians in the window. Then they started coming into the cell room to visit. One day a sweet old couple brought cookies for us, and the jailer was always good about bringing us meals. Sometimes we didn't know just what we were eating, but we ate it anyway. Billy could eat just about anything by holding his nose and shutting his eyes. We all tried doing the same but ended up giggling so hard we couldn't hold our noses.

One morning when we had finished eating our mush, a couple of ladies came to the jail and invited two of us to their home for the day. We were excited to go but also afraid to be separated. I was convinced that I should send Edythe and Violet along together on that first day. They came back that night all prettied up. "We were pampered all day," Edythe said. They were given a bath in a huge bathtub with legs underneath it with water nearly filled to the top. Edythe said that was because they didn't have to carry it in from the creek. There was a pump hooked up right in their kitchen. How about that? They had each been given a new dress and had their hair cut. Wow! Did they ever look different! They each also received a new pair of panties as well as a night dress to wear, and Violet just couldn't keep from dancing that first night back. Both girls kept their new night clothes under the pillow after that.

A few days later the ladies came again to ask for Billy and me. This time one of the men came along to help with Billy. They had to carry him out onto the buckboard to set him up on the front seat. He looked so proud and happy just to be sitting there. We too were taken in and fed a nice home-cooked meal, and then given a bath and new clothes. I got a new pair of panties and a night dress to bring back to the jail to put under my pillow just like Edythe and Violet. Billy slept sound in the jail cell for the first time that night. He'd had only two fits that day. It was so satisfying to have a good bath in a big tub, and we couldn't quite imagine that each of us got to have clean water. We had been taking baths once a week in that old washtub in front of the kitchen stove all our lives with all of us having to share the same water. The littlest one would always be first while the oldest one last, and that was always me. Ugh!

After that, folks would stop by and ask to take us out. They would take us for walks around the town just to show us off, I think. We were rather shy at first, but then it started to be fun because we usually received candy or treats. One fellow even took me into the general store and bought me my first box of Cracker Jacks. I got a tiny rubber doll as a prize when I opened the box. What a surprise! I took it back to the jail and gave it to Violet. She thought she was sitting on top of the world dancing around in circles again with that new dolly cradled in the bend of her elbow.

One morning the newspaper man came to take our pictures standing out in front of the jail. He said he was going to take it back, wherever that was, and put it in his newspaper. I never did hear any more about that photo, nor have I ever seen it.

I don't remember how long we stayed in the Little Falls jail, but one day somebody came to talk to the jailer. The jailer told us later that this guy had gone to the courthouse that morning to decide what to do with us kids. We were told that we were going to be taken for a train ride in the next day or two. We weren't told where, and once again we were terrified wondering what was going to happen to us. We all huddled together and cried. We tried to tell them about Grandma and Grandpa Green living near Merrifield, but they didn't seem to care. *The records show that it was David Willard Green—Grandpa Green—who reported the children abandoned after they had been living alone for nearly two years in the cabin.*

I told them repeatedly about our folks coming back any day now. How would they ever find us again if we weren't there? We were loaded up very early one morning on a train headed south. There were two women with us to hold our hands and try to keep us quiet. They saw to it that we sat still on the hard wooden benches of that train. Billy didn't tolerate the day well at all and seemed particularly scared. He must have suspected early on that he would be taken somewhere different than the rest of us, either because he was a boy or because he was so sick. He cried quietly to himself all the time we were on that train–that is, when he wasn't having his spells.

The train was noisy and smelly with smoke, but I remember that it was a rather interesting trip. The trees were beautiful—all gold and yellow with leaves falling to the ground in the gentle breeze. Flocks of one hundred geese or more were flying the same direction we were traveling. We had sack lunches filled with good things to eat. We were never hungry when we were at that jail or on that train, that's for sure!

We arrived in the big city of Minneapolis, they told us, about noon. Someone took us off the train car, and we walked all around the station. Then we went out a ways and found a tree to sit under. One of the escorts brought us some cold, clear water, which reminded me of the water Edythe and I had to carry from the springs near Owatonna. Soon we were back on another train once more going who knows where.

We got to a town named Faribault in the late afternoon, and some people without suitcases marched boldly into our car and came directly to the two women who were with us. They asked which kids they were to take while they exchanged papers with our escorts. Before we knew it, they had Violet in their arms and they were carrying her away. Then two men took Billy by his arms and started to lead him off the train. The two ladies held Edythe and me back, at which point we all started screaming, kicking, hollering, and wrestling to get away from our captors. It was terrible to say the least! It seemed that in just an instant, Billy and Violet were gone. The train started up again, and we were left behind with never a good-bye or anything. I felt like I'd had my heart cut out of my body, and I was left standing, bleeding, and dying. I looked out of the train window and watched the town disappear along with my beloved brother and sister.

Edythe and I slumped down onto the floor and sobbed ourselves sick. The women tried to comfort us by saying that we would see Violet and Billy again. They said that both of them were being taken to a special school, where Billy would be able to get medicine for his spells. They even promised that Violet would have her ears fixed so she could hear. They kept reassuring us that we would come back soon to visit.

## *Chapter 15*
## *Snuggled Together and Crying*

We were still huddled together on the floor of the train, sobbing, when the train slowed to a stop. We had heard the conductor call, "Owatonna: next stop." Edythe and I were terribly frightened. We both remembered the name from when we had come through this way in the covered wagon, and we said, "Indians!" simultaneously. When the train pulled into the station, we were picked up and dragged off the train by a couple of strange men wearing big black coats and ugly black boots. They plunked us into a buggy and drove us a short distance to a huge building with many windows. I tried to look around to see where we were and noticed a large barn in the background with animals out roaming around in the cow yard. I thought we must be in the country on a farm. But the train had stopped only a short distance down the hill near a town. Strange!

We were taken to the front door of this huge building and ushered up the steps. There Edythe and I were met by a couple of adult women. They carted us down the hall to a small room with two twin beds. There was a small table near the door with two chairs and no windows in the room. The women told us to take our coats off and sit on the bed until they came back. They locked the door behind them when they went out. Edythe said, in-between sobs, that she thought we were in some kind of a prison, which made us cry even harder. What in the world did we ever do that was so terrible? We were left there overnight, and no one came back to check on us. We cried even more when we thought about all the nice clothes we had just gotten from the jail. What would happen to them? We so wanted our new night clothes to put on, but they were never to be seen again. To add to our misery, we had to potty in the worst way, but no one ever came to check on us. We ended up using a large pail in the corner with a cover on it that we had noticed. So we spent the night snuggled together in one bed crying and worrying about Violet and Billy. That was one of the most horrible nights of my entire life, and both Edythe and I had wet the bed by the time morning arrived.

In what we thought must have been morning, they brought us mush and bread on a tray. They said nothing except to eat everything put in front of us or else we would not get another meal. Believe me, we ate every morsel on that tray. We even picked up the crumbs with the spit on our fingertips to make sure they would find nothing left on those trays. We were terrified of what would happen if we disobeyed.

Edythe and I talked long and hard about how we could run away and get back to get Billy and Violet. We didn't quite know where they were, but we had both heard the conductor holler, "Faribault— next stop!" So we thought we knew the town. We were in that room by ourselves for what seemed like a couple of days before they finally brought us nightshirts to sleep in.

Then came the day they led us into a big room that looked like a kitchen. There were large steel tables with lots of cooking kettles hanging around and stoves and sinks over on one side of the room. We were told to stand in line with about twenty other kids that had shown up. I wondered where they had kept them. They told us to take off all our clothes except for our undershirt and panties, which we did rather hesitantly. Thank God, Edythe was standing right behind me, or I don't think I would have cooperated. She slapped me on the side of the head and told me to do what was asked. That was the first time I remember feeling that maybe Edythe was stronger and wiser and that I should listen to her more often.

One by one they took the girls into one room and the boys into another. There they took off all our clothes and stood us in a wash tub and poured green soapy water over our heads. It gagged me and made my eyes burn. They made us sit down in the strange-smelling water and scrubbed me so hard I felt that my skin was going to fall off. They wiped us as dry as one skimpy towel could get us, made us put our undershirt and panties on, and once again we were back standing in line.

A doctor and a dentist were there that day so one by one we were told to sit in the doctor's chair as he examined our ears, eyes, mouth, and privates. I was so scared to have him touch me there I almost peed. After that initial examination, we were allowed to get dressed and proceed to the dentist's chair. The dentist told me I had good teeth. He said, "It doesn't look like you have eaten very much candy." He was right; I hadn't. I felt good about that. Then I went back into the line once more, only to be taken to a cold, steel table and picked up by two more men.

They laid me on my back, and four of the older kids held on to each of my arms and legs. I was spread out like an angel in the snow. One of the men tilted my head over the edge of the table and began to pour a large bucket of kerosene over my hair. It was terrible! The smell was stifling, and he was not very careful how he poured the kerosene. Later they told me that they had done that to get all the head lice and eggs out of my hair. After that I was taken to yet another chair where they cut my hair. This was the worst. This was when I started to cry. I had just had my hair cut by that sweet lady in Little Falls so why were they cutting it again?

After what seemed like forever, I was taken into a different room and given three dresses, three pair of panties, three pairs of long brown cotton stockings with a garter belt to hold them up, and a pair of ugly black shoes. I was also given another nightshirt, so now I had two. I was told to put one set on and carry the other two. Edythe and I were eventually sent on our way with the housemother and taken outside and down the block to our new home, a two-story building with a central hall that housed only girls who were about my own age. There were many bedrooms, with four beds in each room.

Edythe and I were separated for the first time in our lives that day. She was taken to another bedroom farther down the hall. She told me later that her room was on the end and had two windows in it, while mine had only one. She said her room was right next to the door going downstairs and outside so she could run away easier than I could. Together we began planning our future getaway!

*The records show that Sarah and Edythe were admitted to the Owatonna State School for Dependant and Neglected Children on October 8, 1925. Sarah was 13 years old. Officials assigned case numbers to all the children, based on the order in which they arrived at the school. Sarah became #7632 and Edythe became #7633.*

## *Chapter 16*
## *No Whimpering and No Bawling*

Time passed in a blur after that traumatic day of humiliation and separation. I was put in school immediately. Edythe was not in the room with me on the first day, and I worried about that. I found out later that she had been put into another grade that was in a different room. We didn't see each other for days on end. Sometimes I would see her filing out of the dining room after she had eaten when I was just coming in with my group. We were never allowed to wave or talk to one another. It was hard being alone and not knowing what was happening to my siblings. Every time I asked my housemother about visiting Edythe, Billy, or Violet, she scolded me and told me not to bother her. She said she didn't know anything so I should quit asking her.

I cried myself to sleep often at night under the sheets. If we were ever heard, we were taken out of our beds, spanked with a radiator brush in front of all the other girls, and sent back to bed with instructions: "No whimpering and no more bawling!" I only had to go through that treatment once before I had it figured out never to cry so anyone could hear me.

We were taken to a special room on Sundays where we heard the preachers and teachers tell us all about a Jesus who lived in heaven. They taught us how to pray to Him about our problems and told us things would get better. After that, I prayed every night for Jesus to take care of Billy and Violet. I asked Him to tell them not to cry, and He should let them know that I was coming to get them real soon. He became my rock of hope and strength after that. He was my buddy and friend. I went to sleep knowing there was someone I could talk to about my troubles, and He would keep them a secret. I remember teaching myself the Lord's Prayer while in bed waiting to fall asleep, and I tried to sing some of the church songs under my breath too.

We were sent to bed at 7:30 every night, summer or winter. It was hard in the summer because it was still light outside, and we simply were not tired. I tried everything to entertain myself until I fell asleep. It was then that I taught myself how to twiddle my thumbs under the sheets, of course. I even practiced wiggling my toes one at a time while not moving the others. I kept up this routine until I started working in the kitchen as a pantry girl. My duties gave me more freedom coming and going from building to building and permission to stay up later after bedtime.

We were often taken to the kitchen after school and taught how to set the table and serve the teachers. I was dressed up in a white uniform with an apron and taught how to walk and talk with dishes in my hands. I was given lesson after lesson on how to pass plates and serve bowls of food and how to pick up empty bowls from the center of the table while standing behind the left shoulder of the adult at the table. Eventually, I was given the job of serving the teachers in their own special dining room, away from the rest of the kids and their tables.

I really enjoyed my job. For the first time in my life, I felt like I was worth something and proud to be doing a good job. I kept getting positive comments on how good I was and how well I was doing. I felt good about myself for the first time in my life. I worked at this from six in the morning until it was time to go to school and again after school in the evening until we finished cleaning up the dining room. I was privileged not to have to clean the floors on my hands and knees as the other kids who helped had to do. Then I changed into my regular clothes, returned to my dormitory, and reported to my housemother or else reported to my classroom for school. This became my regular routine while I was at the orphanage. Sometimes—but not often—I would be called in early after school to help with the kitchen work when there was something special happening.

As time went on, I was given extra duties in the kitchen. One such duty was the chore of feeding the "naughty" kids who were kept in the tower. This was the first time I realized there were even stronger punishments for especially naughty kids. Seeing this devastated me. Before long I was taught how to carry trays of mush that were delivered every morning and evening. I had to learn how to go up and down the stairs with the trays, trying not to spill or drop them. I was small and agile enough never to have any kind of a bad fall and was often praised about how quick I was at getting my duties done. This made me try to work even faster. I was never allowed to speak to any of the kids. They told me if I did I would be beaten and taken off my job, never to serve again. I realized how serious this was, but when I saw some terrible-looking bodies and faces, I could not keep from asking questions. I whispered to them trying to give some comfort. I sneaked hankies or napkins from the tables I was serving and took them to the kids.

The tower they were kept in was a tall, round building of its own built right on the side of the front entry. No one hardly ever noticed it was there because it looked like it was just part of the building. But inside were floors almost the size of a silo. There was a pail of water in one area to drink from with only one common dipper for all to use. On the other side of the tower was a bucket to use when relieving oneself. Kids with major and minor offenses were kept there. When we got the chance, they told me how they got there. They said they had talked back to the teacher or had hit or gotten into a fight with another kid. Then, if or when they were taken to the headmaster, they were beaten with a strap or belt. They would end up with terrible black eyes or bruises all over their bodies. Then they were put in the tower while they healed or repented. Most were boys, but I remember a few girls there too. The first time I saw Edythe in the tower I fell to my knees, and we both bawled. She had answered the teacher with a dirty word and had her mouth slapped. Then she yelled back with even more profanity so she was sent to the headmaster. He slapped her across the mouth and face to chase the bad language out, he told her. She was there more than a week to heal.

It was not unusual to hear how one kid or another had tried to run away, had been caught, taken back to be whipped, and put in the tower. I found in the coming year that I'd see Edythe there every month or so. She had even tried to run away a couple of times but was caught. Once she tried to get sexy and offered the headmaster her body so he wouldn't whip her. Then she got it worse than ever. I cried for days seeing her beaten so badly. I would hide extra bread or a cracker in my apron pocket to take to her hoping to make her heal faster. Why I was never caught I will never understand.

After this experience with the tower, I became more acutely aware of some of the kids that I saw with healing wounds and black eyes as well as sore backs. I was more compassionate than ever toward them. I would sneak some kind of snack from the dining room to pass to them when we met in the hall. I always tried to be the last one into my bed at night so I could sneak some kind of a favor to some of the more poorly treated girls. It seemed like a few were picked on more than others by the housemother or the teachers.

There was always embarrassment and ridicule for those who wet their beds. They had to remove their sheets in the morning, wash them in the sink by hand, put them out on the clothesline, and stand next to the bed clothes all day waiting for them to dry. The kids who walked by jeered without any comment from the housemother. I was often subjected to this particular type of cruelty. I had a habit of wetting the bed, especially when I was upset about my siblings or when Edythe was in the tower. I just knew what the next morning would bring. Sometimes I tried to stay awake all night so I wouldn't have an accident. When I had one, it would mean no school or work that day as I spent the day under the clothesline waiting for my sheets to dry.

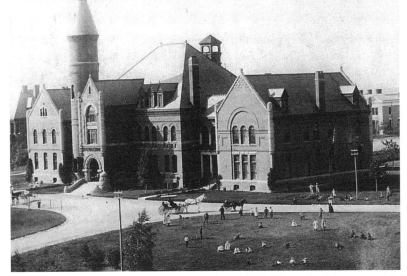

*State School for Dependent and Neglected Children in Owatonna, MN*

# Chapter 17
## The Tunnel

*I feel I must make clear once more at the start of this chapter that this is the story my mother told me when I was a child and often later in my life. I have researched this issue, but I have found no documentation or mention anywhere of children shackled at the Owatonna orphanage. Groups of volunteer investigators have gone down into the tunnel and found indentations in the walls at various places, where newer cement has been filled in to repair former holes, where chains could have possibly been drilled into the cement wall long ago.*

As time went on, I was given more and more duties. It was then that I found out about the tunnel under the buildings going from one building to another. I never knew anything like that existed until the head kitchen matron told me she was going to train me to take meals down to the tunnel. I followed her a couple of times, and to my horror I saw kids, both boys and girls, shackled to the side walls. They were suffering from terrible injuries but had received no treatment that I could detect. My job was to give them their mush and bread in the morning and again in the evening. I was informed there was to be no talking and no contact of any kind. I was not to tell anyone what I saw nor was I EVER to speak to anyone about my duties in the tunnel. If it was discovered that I had broken this unwritten rule, I would be severely punished, taken out of school, and never allowed to work at my job again. They threatened that I would get the kind of beating the kids in the tunnel had received and would be sent to do time right alongside them. I was so traumatized from all I had seen and heard that first day that I wept and shook uncontrollably under my blankets that night. I knew I would wet the bed and have horrible nightmares if I let myself sleep.

The next Monday I started bringing food to the tunnel on a regular basis. I was watched like a hawk every time I went down there. For weeks someone followed me into the shadows to make sure I didn't have any verbal contact with those kids. I saw broken arms, legs, cuts, and open wounds that needed medical attention. There were some down there who seemed to have been there for a long time. They looked at me with hollow, sunken eyes and cowered as far away from me as the shackle would allow so they wouldn't have to look me in the eye or have me accidentally touch them. I delivered mush in the morning, leaving the dishes behind to pick up in the evening when I brought in another bowl. After about a week or so of constant watching, I was allowed to go alone once in awhile, and eventually they trusted me with the entire responsibility. When I felt confident that I was not being spied on, I attempted to smile, make eye contact, or even touch their frail bodies. I often saw heaps of body waste, but someone must have come down every so often and cleaned up the mess. There was always a stench when they opened the kitchen door leading down to the inner door of the tunnel at the bottom of the steps. Now I knew why they always kept that part of the back kitchen shut off from the rest of the room.

I finally got the courage to ask one bright-eyed boy who had two terribly mangled legs what had happened to him. He smiled and said, "I ran away one time too often or should I say I got caught one time too often." They had beaten him with a sledge hammer, crushing both his legs. I doubted if he would ever heal properly. He told me that he had been in the tunnel for a long time. After that I whispered to him as often as I felt it was safe. I told him what day it was, what the weather was like, and reported what I had done in school that day. It would make him smile just to see me come in the tunnel.

I felt terribly sorry for him but not as sorry as I did for the little colored girl who was shackled next to him. Eventually she started to talk to me too. She said she was 11 years old and had gotten pregnant by one of the teachers. I found out she was turning 12 soon, so I kept track of the days until her birthday came. Then I sneaked a sugar cookie down to her in my apron pocket. She cried when I gave it to her. She broke the cookie in half and told me to give the other half to the boy with the broken legs. That sugar cookie seemed to bring her a little happiness on her birthday.

I knew when it was about time for her to deliver her baby. She was so miserable sitting on that hard, cold, cement floor. The memory of her sitting there shackled to the wall so late into her pregnancy is something I will never forget. I became more and more angry with the big wigs who ran this insane place. I grew up in a hurry that year.

I constantly tried to figure out ways to make things better for all the innocent kids being forced to endure such inhumane treatment. I took the evening mush down one night and found Lily (not her real name) in labor. I immediately went back up and whispered into the head matron's ear what I knew. She took a step or two back, looked me square in the eye, and said, "Now don't you worry about that little black girl. She will do just fine. Those folks know how to have their babies without any help. There is no need to mention this to anyone. She will take care of herself. Now you get on with the rest of your chores and say nothing to anyone else or you know what will happen to you, right?"

I did as I was told, and when I finished cleaning up that night, I took off my uniform and apron and hung them where they belonged.

But instead of going out the main door, I quickly ducked through the tunnel door. I sat with Lily for a couple of hours helping her bear her pain as well as I knew how. She was having a terrible time. Lily, the boy next to her, and I all sat and cried together. It was getting late, and I knew that the matron would be leaving the building soon. She always locked the kitchen door when she left so I had to say good-bye and leave just as quietly as I came in. I sneaked back into my room and went to bed with my clothes on. I was up late enough to pee before I slept so I was lucky not to wet the bed that night.

I awoke very early the next morning, left my bed, and went to the kitchen. The door was open so I sneaked down to the tunnel again to check on Lily. She was gone! I asked the boy with the broken legs what had happened and he said, "Well, she just quit screaming." He said they had come down to check on her and then carried her away. There was still a mess on the floor where she had been sitting. I left crying my heart out. I wondered if they had finally taken her to the hospital on the orphanage grounds. One building was for the kids under a certain age and the other was for the older ones. I found out later that day when I asked another girl who worked at the hospital that Lily had never arrived there. She had not heard or seen anything of her. I figured then that Lily had probably just died when she quit screaming. It was not the policy when I was at the orphanage to have funerals for the kids who died. They were just taken away to the hospital morgue and never heard of again.

I often noticed that sometimes in the early darkness of night there was a commotion going on down the path that led to the cemetery. If I peeked out the window near my bed, I saw men carrying a coffin and setting it down near some newly dug hole. That evening I finished my chores just in time to notice goings-on down the path to the cemetery, so I followed the men carrying the coffin and watched them set it down near the hole. I asked one of them if it was a little colored girl, and they replied, "How would you know that?" I never answered them but turned and ran back toward my building. One of the men chased me, grabbed my arm, and turned me in to my housemother. I was whipped severely with the radiator brush and taken to the headmaster. He had already retired for the night so that probably saved me from another whipping. But I was put in the tower for five days for breaking the rules. If I broke the rules again they told me next time it would be for ten days.

I bawled the whole time I was in the tower. I was devastated to think that no one came to help Lily when she needed it the most. And why was an 11-year-old girl pregnant in the first place? I grieved for her, felt sorry for myself, sorry for Edythe getting into so much trouble, and was terribly lonesome for Billy and Violet. The feelings came tumbling down on me all at once, and I cried harder than I have ever cried in my whole life. It was then and there, during those five days in the tower, that I decided I must do something, somehow, to find Billy and Violet.

*Crackers and Milk*

## Chapter 18
## *Washing Their Heads With Kerosene*

I went back to school and my job as soon as I was released from the tower, but I was treated very badly by my house matron and others in the kitchen. I wasn't allowed to talk to anyone. I was told to walk with my head down and look no one in the face. They slammed doors in my face whenever they had the chance, and I believe they intentionally stepped on my shoes. It forced me to polish my shoes all over again as they had to pass inspection every day before going to work. The others walked behind me and messed up my place settings just when I had finished laying them out, and I would have to start setting all over again.

I wasn't allowed to go back into the tunnel for quite a while until one evening my house matron yelled, "I'm getting sick and tired of doing your dirty work for you! Here—you take this tray down to the tunnel yourself." She practically threw it at me. From then on I was allowed to go back to my regular duties. But once again, they watched me closely for a long time to make sure I wasn't talking to any of the "inmates."

I went to the superintendent soon after that to make an appointment to talk about visiting Billy and Violet. He told me that I would have to do lots of things before he would consider it. He mentioned that I would have to get better grades at school, take on extra chores to earn my way over there, and stay out of trouble for three months. Then, he said, he would consider it. I was so depressed. Three months was a long time, and Christmas was coming.

*Crackers and Milk*

As I cleaned up the dining room one evening, I found a catalog on the chair that had been left behind by one of the teachers. I put it in my pocket to read later. It was a catalog filled with things you could order by mail. I was so excited when I found a corn husk doll for 59 cents. "How wonderful for Violet," I thought. There was also a watch for $1.29 for Billy. I knew instantly that these were the presents I wanted to give to them for Christmas. But how and where was I ever going to get $1.88?

One evening when I was changing my uniform, I overheard the kitchen help complaining about always having to work on Saturdays and Sundays. They mentioned that they would even pay someone to wash pots and pans if they could find such a person. I got really bold and spoke up, "Hey! I will wash the pots and pans if you want me to." They turned around with quite a surprised look when they saw me standing there. They looked at one another and winked. They quietly told me what to do and how to do it. They said to keep track of the count, and they would pay me one penny a pan. I skipped and jumped all the way back to my room that evening. I was thrilled! I had figured out a way to buy the Christmas presents for my brother and sister.

I worked hard after that, every weekend, in the kitchen washing pots and pans. But I didn't care. I sang, whistled, and washed—all the while counting. I soon had my $2.00 to send in my order and pay for postage as well. And I was working extra jobs to make it look good for the superintendent.

It didn't take long before they even asked me to come in on Saturday afternoons to help bring in the new kids. This was the only day of the week that they brought in new "inmates," as they called them. They were all treated the same way Edythe and I had been when we first arrived. I helped out wherever they needed me for a while, and before too long they started making me stand at the steel table to help hold down kids while they washed their heads with kerosene. It was then that I had another bout with death.

There were two Indian brothers who had come in that day. One was about 5 or 6 and the other was younger. They were just as scared and anxious as I had been. They didn't seem to understand anything that was happening. The little boys had to be tied in both the doctor's and dentist's chairs to be examined. They made some awful growling noises all the while and fought every inch of the way as they went along. Then it was time to put them on the table for the kerosene. The staff lifted the youngest one up first. He fought so hard that no matter how hard we tried, we could not hold him still enough to get the kerosene aimed just right. The staff kept blaming us kids for not holding him tight enough. We couldn't find any way to hold the little boy that kept him quiet.

Then the staff came flying at all four of us kids screaming profanities and hit us with the backs of their hands upside the head, knocking us all to the floor. Finally someone got hold of the superintendent, and he sent two big strong men who came marching into the room. I noticed they were wearing the same black ugly boots that I had seen at the train station. They picked up that little fellow and slammed him so hard onto the table that he let out such a blood-curdling scream that all the kids standing in line started to scream and cry! They had to hold his older brother back from the table. I think it took about three big guys to hold him down.

They continued to pour kerosene all over his head until he quit screaming. Then everything became quiet like in church. No one moved. Not even the little Indian kid on the table. No one said a word. One of big guys picked him up and carried him out with his arms and legs dangling. He was covered completely with kerosene that slopped all over as he went. We never saw him again, and I watched that night to see if they took another little coffin to the cemetery. I spent another sleepless night trying not to wet myself.

## Chapter 19
### *Little Ones Left in Boxes*

After that I became more acquainted with Margaret, a girl in my class who worked in the hospital after school. I asked her if she knew of any jobs I could get there. She explained that there was work, but I had to get permission from the superintendent to start. And when I thought about it more, there really was no time for me to work in the hospital, with my chores in the kitchen, dining room, tower, and tunnel. I felt bad because I knew that it was something I would really like to do when Margaret explained all of her different duties. She saw lots of sick kids — many who eventually died. I mentioned that I watched for them to be taken to the cemetery but never saw the procession. She told me that not all of them were buried at our cemetery; some were taken elsewhere. When kids came into the orphanage, they would be examined, and if they were found to be sick, they were taken to the hospital right away, probably before they were registered.

She said that some of the babies were too sick to be helped and some had contagious diseases. These babies were often put out on the porch in a box away from the other patients. Then the staff shut the door and waited for them to die. Margaret said it was really hard to work knowing all this, but she was told never to talk about it to anyone. If she did, she would be punished and sent to the tower. We ended up telling each other secrets like this every Saturday night when we took our baths. We were all lined up and two at a time would bathe together in the tub. This procedure was supposed to save time as well as water. She washed my back and I washed hers. We often got scolded and slapped around because we spent too much time talking while bathing. We got so that we didn't care how much they batted us around, we still could hardly wait until Saturday night came when we could be together again.

Often after that, I would sneak over to the hospital and try to find out if there were any little ones left in boxes. I sneaked through the laundry room back door, up the stairs, and onto the porch, where I sat on the floor and held those tiny ones in my arms. I sang to them and tried to comfort them by sticking my little finger into their mouths. I never knew their names so I named them myself. I remember one I named Rose and one I called Elizabeth. One tiny one I named Jeremiah from the Bible.

I prayed to my Jesus often that He would watch over them when I wasn't there. I asked Him to take them home to His heaven when they died. Then I would sit and cry. Often they were too sick to cry so I simply held them in my arms. I had to put them back into the box and leave when it started to get dark. Usually they were gone by the next night when I went back to check. I now believe it was a miracle that I never got sick or picked up any of those diseases they were said to have had. Jesus must have been watching over me. The hardest time to go visit the porch was in winter. I left tracks in the snow, and the help at the hospital started talking. Margaret warned me, and I had to stay away. I often wonder now why I was never discovered.

## *Chapter 20*
## *There Is Only One Way*

As Christmas approached, I asked for help from one of the kitchen matrons to order presents for my family. We picked my three favorite items from the catalog, and she had the items sent to her. She said she would keep them until I needed them. I went back often to try to make another appointment with the superintendent so I could plan a holiday visit with Violet and Billy. He turned me away, but I kept going back. I was so lonesome for my little brother and sister. I hadn't heard a thing from them since they were taken off the train in Faribault.

I kept trying to formulate a plan to persuade the superintendent to let me go for a visit. I had done everything he asked, even the most ridiculous request of all, to read six books and send him the book reports. I was getting good grades in school, I was never late for my chores, and I was asked to take on more duties in the dining hall. I was told to come to the kitchen an hour before it opened and sweep the walkway. As winter came, I shoveled snow too, getting up at 4:30 in the morning. I now taught new girls the dining room serving routine. As far as I know, no one but me was ever trained to take trays to the tower or the tunnel. I think, now that I am older, this is why my requests were denied to go to the gym for swimming and other sports after school when most girls had privileges. I was always needed in the dining halls, tower, and tunnel to do my dirty work. I think that they did everything possible to keep me from bonding with other girls as they were afraid I might start talking. When I wet the bed and wasn't allowed on duty those days, the house matron had to do my chores. She let me know time and time again how much she didn't appreciate it.

In late fall I started begging for appointments to see the superintendent. They were always denied. Christmas came and went. I thought about what to do for a long time and decided the only way to press my point was to go on a hunger strike. What else could I do? Doing what the superintendent asked hadn't done me any good; he simply rewarded me by adding more duties to my already full routine.

One Sunday, soon after Christmas, when my Sunday meal was offered, I refused. The staff looked surprised and asked me if I was sick. I told them that I wasn't going to eat anything until I could visit Billy and Violet. My house matron shook me up pretty badly and sent me back to my room for the rest of the day. I was told to think about what I was doing. I was rather scared by this time, but I had made up my mind I was going to go ahead with the hunger strike, and nothing was going to stop me. No supper was brought to me that night, but I still reported for my regular duties the next morning. Not a word was said, but when they set my breakfast down in front of me, I pushed it back. I finished my chores, changed into my regular clothes, and went to school. I refused both lunch and supper that day as well. I remember being hungry and having a headache, but I knew I was just stubborn enough to hold the course.

Everyone seemed to ignore me the first day, but when the superintendent came into the dining room that evening, he asked to talk to me, and I knew I was in trouble. He pulled me aside and scolded me. He was so angry he spit in my face while yelling at me and shook his finger so hard he scratched my face. I went back to my chores in tears but more determined than ever. I told him just that the next day when he pulled me into his office and shoved me into his big red velvet chair.

When he finished yelling and screaming at me, I yelled and screamed just as loud back at him. We both stood up about to go into battle when he suddenly quit yelling. He took a step back, stood straight at attention, and said, "Sarah, there is only one way I can see that this problem will be resolved, and that is to put you in the tower so you have time to think." And off I went to the tower. Before I went in, they tore off my uniform and apron and asked me to remove my panties, shoes, and stockings. This was the most embarrassing moment of all. I was left standing there with nothing on but an under slip that had come with the uniform. I realied there was no going back. I was in for a long battle.

I still refused to eat when they brought the mush or bread, but I did drink. I got so dizzy that I had funny dreams. I felt terrible. I was beginning to think I was probably going to die, but I didn't care; I wanted to visit my family. Kids came and went, but I stayed. Every day I was hauled back into the superintendent's office. I was too dirty to sit on the red velvet chair so they brought in a wooden chair, and I sat on that. I refused to listen to anything he said. I just held my head down and looked at the floor. He told me a tube would be stuck down my throat to force-feed me if I didn't start eating soon. That really scared me.

Not long after that, the two men with ugly black boots came abruptly into the tower and dragged me down the steps. They handed me some panties, shoes, and a dress and yelled at me to put them on. Then they grabbed me by my arm and dragged me out to a waiting buggy. I was forced onto the floor of the back seat, and a horse blanket was thrown over me. It had to have been the coldest day on record that winter because I don't remember being that cold again in my entire life. I was bounced around so badly that I was black and blue on my rear end and elbows for weeks. When the horse blanket was pulled off, I was in front of a big building. I was dragged into an office and forced to sit in another big red velvet chair. I soon realized that I was probably in Faribault near Billy and Violet. I started asking a thousand questions. The man there was very polite and quiet spoken, and he talked to me a long time about my trip. He told me that he had heard how badly I had wanted to see my brother and sister. A lady came in with a glass of milk and two sugar cookies and offered them to me. I took them rather savagely and ate to my heart's content but felt rather embarrassed when I finished. I noticed that the man was watching me intently and seemed to be smiling to himself.

They proceeded to tell me all about Violet and said that they would bring her to visit in this office. I was so excited. I think I asked to go to the toilet at least a dozen times. Finally, Violet was escorted into the room by the hand of a matron. She looked more beautiful than I had ever seen her. She was cleanly dressed, and her hair was neatly done up with a ribbon. She looked so pretty! I hugged her so hard she let out a scream because she couldn't breathe. Then I remembered that I hadn't brought any of the Christmas presents along. I felt so bad I cried, but we sat and played on the floor all afternoon. It warmed my heart just to be close enough to touch her. They brought in games and dolls as well as a paper doll book, but we had to ask for scissors. For our meal, we were given a bowl of soup, crackers, and another glass of milk. We had so much fun crushing the crackers into our milk and eating them. It had been a long time since I had tasted this delicious food. The afternoon slipped away fast, but I felt connected to my family again. I felt bad, though, that I hadn't asked for Edythe to be there too. I cried about it all the way home, freezing in the back of that buggy.

## Chapter 21
## *The Visit*

That afternoon ended way too soon when the men with ugly black boots came to tell me it was time to leave. I wondered why they hadn't brought Billy, and when I asked about him, they said, "Never mind Billy, we have to leave now before it gets too dark!" Someone came to get Violet, and they led her out of the room with not even a good-bye. But I insisted, before we left, that we talk once more to the kind man who was in charge to ask about Billy. I started to get loud about wanting to talk him when the men grabbed me by my elbows and carried me out to the waiting buggy. I kicked, screamed, and wrestled myself away. I ran ahead and crawled under the team of horses. I got between the horses and hung on to the tongue of the buggy, upside down, with all my strength. The men tried their hardest to reach me, but the horses kept sidestepping and prancing around. The men were afraid of getting hurt so they stepped back and started yelling for help.

The professor came out to see what all the commotion was about, and the men left to go get a helper from the barn to come and quiet the horses while another crawled between the horses to retrieve a yelling, kicking kid. It was then that the kind professor asked the men to bring me back to his office. They did so, rudely, and plunked me, once again, into the big red velvet chair. After the professor asked the men to leave, he proceeded to tell me in his quiet, mild manner why Billy hadn't come to visit. He said that Billy had become very ill in November and had been taken to the hospital and was still too ill to have visitors.

I gasped and thought, "How could that be? He was as healthy as could be when he got off that train. What did they do to him? Why hadn't Edythe and I been notified? How long was he sick? When could I go to see him?" There were so many questions.

The two men came into the room, took me by the arms, and walked me out to the buggy. They covered me with the horse blanket and slowly drove away. I sobbed all the way back to town and through the night with my head under the covers. I was never allowed to go back to visit. Billy died later that same year, and Edythe and I were never informed of his death. It wasn't until after I turned 18 and was able to go back to Faribault for a visit that I found out he had died, and then no one could or would tell me where he was buried. It was almost 60 years before that information was given to me. I did not see Violet for another 15 years.

**Billy and Violet in Faribault**

## Chapter 22
## A Family from Fergus Falls

The rest of the winter went by without any further incidents; still I seemed to walk around in a daze. I kept asking for appointments to see about visiting Violet and checking on Billy, but to no avail.

I was an outcast with the kitchen help as well as my teacher and housemother, but I didn't care. What difference did it make? I was so depressed about Billy's illness. I kept thinking how Jesus and I were going to make everything right when I got out of this God-forsaken place, but how was it ever going to be right for Billy? My depression must have been terrible during that long, cold winter because I was constantly being called in for not keeping up with my schoolwork. I was often punished for being late for my chores in the dining room. I turned very coldhearted that winter. Nothing mattered anymore.

Somehow spring came anyway. I reminisced about that old blue sweater with a hole in the elbow when I went to school for the first time without my coat. As I meandered along the sidewalk, I wondered whatever happened to Ollie. I wondered about my dad as well as my mother and Dorothy. I decided the next time I talked to the superintendent I would ask him to help me look for them.

In April when the superintendent called me into his office, I was excited because I thought we were going to plan another visit to Faribault. Once more I sat on that big red velvet chair and waited for him to come into the room. He shuffled some papers around when he took my hand and shook it, something he had never done before. He proceeded to tell me about a letter he had received regarding a family from Fergus Falls, last name Boyum, who needed a girl to help out in their home, and he thought of me.

I had been in lineups many times in the past to see if someone would get chosen to go with a family. Usually it happened on a Sunday. We were told to keep our Sunday dresses on and report to the big hall. We realized this was another "viewing" of the girls. Someone came to look us over and then decided if they wanted to take one of us. This was common practice, and we'd always get excited thinking that maybe, just maybe, this would be the day to get out of this place. I was never picked. Maybe it was because of my red hair or my record of being naughty. And I was smaller and frailer than other girls my age, and it always seemed hard for me to smile. I even imagined it was because I had turned 14 in March and was too old to be placed. So why was I talked to, personally, about being placed in a home? The superintendent explained that the family could not come to Owatonna to pick a girl because the woman was too ill, and the man wouldn't leave her behind. So the superintendent was to pick one, and he chose me.

I was so thrilled that I skipped all the way back to my building. It wasn't until after I had crawled into bed that evening that I thought about leaving Edythe behind. How was I going to get to see her to tell her, and what would she think of all this? I had so many questions to ask, but they would have to wait. Weeks went by before I heard any more. I heard the teachers talking about the measles epidemic at the orphanage. They were even thinking of closing the school.

*The records show that a letter was sent to the Boyum family of Fergus Falls stating that there was a measles epidemic at the orphanage. It said that Sarah would be sent as soon as the quarantine was lifted.*

Finally, in May, the call came for me to pack my things and report to the front office. I was given only one hour's notice before I was to leave for my new home. I never got to say good-bye to Edythe or Margaret.

I was delivered to my new home in a car and told that my responsibilities were to do housework and care for the baby. As it turned out, there were four other kids in the family besides the baby as well as a very sick mother, but I was delighted to be working with little ones. This job was going to be fun, I thought. But I wasn't there an hour before I realized it was not going to be easy or fun. They spoke another language, Norwegian, and I couldn't understand a thing they said. Worst of all, they kept pulling my hair! What was wrong with these people?

I tried to make the best of it all by being friendly and doing more than they asked of me. The mother was so sick she left just about everything for me to do that summer. I was happy to be back in a home again, but it wasn't easy. There were too many chores that needed doing with such a big family. I never had enough time to get them all finished. The mother and father never took me anywhere because I couldn't speak the language. At least that is what they told me. It was hard to be left behind when they would go to church or out visiting on Sundays. There was always a list of chores for me to do while they were gone. I got so lonesome on those days I cried.

*Crackers and Milk*

I wasn't there very long when they told me that I would be going back to the Owatonna orphanage. I had mixed feelings about this, but I knew it was for the best as I wasn't exactly happy there either. I returned to the orphanage in September that year, just in time to start my new class at school.

I found out later that the orphanage had received a letter from the family. They had decided they wanted a girl who could speak Norwegian. They also insisted that the new one chosen not have red hair. For the first time in my life I felt different because of my auburn hair.

# Chapter 23
# Prepare for Placement

I was hardly back at the orphanage two weeks when I was given notice to dress and appear for another placement lineup. I dressed and walked unenthusiastically to the main hall, not in any hurry this time. "What's the use," I thought, "who would want this 'thing' with red hair anyway?" Besides, I still hadn't been able to see or talk to Edythe about my adventures of the past months with the Boyum family.

I arrived late so I was placed in the back row, where I stood fidgeting with the hem of my dress, which heightened my awareness of its length. It seemed to have gotten very short that summer. I didn't even notice that there were two people stopped in front of me who were whispering to one another. I was taken by the shoulder and asked to turn around slowly. I was rather startled but did as I was told. They proceeded to ask me a few questions. This had never happened to me before in a lineup. They continued on, but when it was announced that we could all file out of the room, they asked me and another girl to stay. Was I surprised! Once again they questioned me about my age and grades in school. They even asked if I liked children and would feel comfortable with a farm family. I told them yes. They asked me what size clothing I wore. How was I to know? I had never noticed size when the clothes were handed out. The matron in charge answered for me. We were told to leave the room but to wait in the hall, which we did.

It seemed to take forever before they came out to say that they had picked me. I didn't know whether to laugh or cry. I was so afraid that what had happened at the Boyums would happen again.

I was told to return to my room and wait for further orders. I went back to my building but heard nothing the rest of that evening. The next day I returned to school and work with this dilemma still on my mind. But within a few days I received notice to prepare for my placement the following Sunday.

Again, I was worried about how to get the news to Edythe. I asked some of my friends at school to let her know that I would write to her as soon as I possibly could. This time I asked for addresses, stamps, and envelopes before I left.

Mr. Eigen *(not his real name)* came alone that day in early October to pick me up in a buggy. I was 14 years old and felt no remorse leaving this place once more. I only felt sadness at leaving Edythe behind. But I took a second to pray for the kids locked in the tower and, worse yet, those shackled in the tunnel. Then I rode off down the driveway on my way to another adventure!

*I asked Sarah later in life, "Mom, why do you think they picked you?"*

*She said, "I think it was because they had clothes my size already at their place that were hand-me-downs from their daughter.*

## *Chapter 24*
## *Mr. Eigen and the New Family*

Mr. Eigen and I rode in a horse-drawn buggy most of that day to get to their farm, which was near Kenyon, Minnesota, about 20 miles away. It was cold and windy with gray skies. We talked a lot about different things as we went along. I felt it was necessary that Mr. Eigen understand how important it was for me to go see Billy in Faribault. I told him about my experience with my last visit. I even asked him when we could plan this trip. He answered me by saying, "We came for you to help us on our farm with all the work. We don't have time to be running you all over the countryside visiting relatives." Already I was feeling disappointed with the situation.

Mr. Eigen spoke of his family. He said he had a wife, two sons and a daughter. The boys were around my age, and the girl was younger. He also mentioned that the bedrooms were full, but he and his wife had decided I could sleep in the attic room above the porch for now. What he didn't mention was that the attic room had no windows, was not high enough to stand up in and was not heated. So on very cold winter nights, they let me sleep on the floor behind the kitchen stove. In the summer, when it was hot, I slept in the upper room above the milkhouse. It was not as big, but it had a little window for better circulation than there was in the room above the porch. I had to crawl up on a stepladder attached to the inside wall and into a hole on the floor of the little space.

Mr. Eigen spelled out the rules that I had to follow while in his home. One important rule was that I could not speak unless I was spoken to.

That bothered me as I was one who enjoyed a good conversation. I knew this was going to be a hard test to pass. I was not allowed to eat with the family but would prepare their meals and then step out of the room while the family ate. I learned to survive on "leftovers" that the dog didn't get. I also learned, through the years, to nibble and taste a good deal as I was preparing the food.  In the summer I often stole from the garden. I was so thankful that I had my crackers and milk to rely on! I asked Mr. Eigen to buy crackers whenever I needed them, and he always obliged. He told me he thought that was a good snack for me. I always had fresh milk from the cows so I never went to bed hungry.

Mr. Eigen forewarned me that Mrs. Eigen was a hard woman to satisfy and that obeying her was going to be the hardest rule of all to follow. He mentioned that her little girl, Mary (*not her real name*), was a favorite child, and she wanted the best for her. He said the main reason they had gotten me from the orphanage was to help with the work in place of Mary. Mrs. Eigen wanted Mary to grow up knowing the elegant way of life and didn't want her to suffer doing all the menial chores that were required on a farm. She taught her how to play the piano and to embroider with fine thread. Mary was to be dressed appropriately at all times. Mr. Eigen rambled on and on about his little girl being raised to fit into the higher class of society. I began to realize just where my place was in this family—very close to the bottom of the ladder.

I thought we would never reach our destination. It was dark when we finally turned in to the driveway. Mr. Eigen asked me to help him unload the wagon, which didn't sound bad because I had only one bag. But what he meant was that I was to help him unhitch the horses and get them in the barn. This was something I had never done before.

I was nervous but brave and did as I was told. I never let on that I was new at unhitching horses. I watched him undo his side of the harness, and then I did the same on my side. "Good job!" he said. He carried his load into the tack room, and I tried to do the same, but the harness was too heavy so I dragged it along the ground. He chuckled a bit at my effort and came to help me lift the harness up onto the nails. I noticed how dirty my best dress was from carrying the tack, and I tried to wipe it off as we went into the house. I was also shivering as my thin coat had not been much help keeping me warm.

Mrs. Eigen was waiting for us at the kitchen door. She had prepared hot mush and coffee. This was the first time I had ever tasted coffee. I was never allowed to drink any when I was in Fergus Falls or the orphanage. As far as I was concerned, I wouldn't miss it if I was never to taste it again. But it was hot and warmed my tummy so that I quit shivering.

When we were finished eating, I was taken to my tiny room above the porch. It had a small hand-built bed with a feather tick pillow and a very old homemade quilt. There I put my bag down, and they shut the door tight as they announced I would be awakened at 5 a.m. to help make breakfast and meet the family.

I was alone, as in the past, and felt very apprehensive about my tomorrows at this place. I was afraid to sleep as I was worried about wetting the bed. I don't remember putting my head on the pillow. I awoke with the same clothes on as the night before, including my coat. It was still dark, and they hadn't called me yet, so I struggled in this close space to get my older dress out of the bag and slip it on. My good dress was filthy from the chores the night before. I had to kneel on my knees to dress. About that time, Mrs. Eigen opened the door and found me sitting on the side of the bed all dressed for the day.

She ushered me into the kitchen and showed me where all the pots and pans and dishes were kept. She told me to set the table and showed me how to cook the mush just the way the family liked it. They cooked it with milk instead of water. She taught me how to make the coffee just the way they wanted it. When breakfast was ready, I was told to wait out on the porch behind closed doors while the family ate.

After they had eaten, they called me into the kitchen and introduced me to the family. No words were exchanged, only shy looks of discontent from the boys. Mary hadn't awakened yet. Mr. Eigen told me to get ready and come to the barn with him as there were chores to do. I was about to put on my thin coat when he handed me a pair of bib overalls and an oversized black coat. He told me these were my winter barn clothes and to only wear them in the barn. I followed him around for the next couple of hours and watched what he was doing. He talked to me only when there was something to explain. The boys stayed behind in the house to get ready for school. When we finished getting the cattle in from the barnyard, he showed me how he milked the cows. He was amazed to see that I already knew how to milk a cow. I never did get to explain to him how I had learned that technique.

We fed the horses their morning hay and put them out to pasture, and then it was on to feed the chickens and pigs. After all this was finished, I was allowed to go back into the kitchen and clean up the breakfast table and dishes.

After cleanup, Mr. Eigen showed me how they cleaned the wooden kitchen floor. They took wood ashes from the ash tray of the stove and sprinkled them over the surface of the floor. Then I had to get down on my hands and knees and scrub the ashes into the wood with a large scrub brush. When I was finished, I was to sweep the ashes into a pile, put them into a dust pan, and carry them out to the garden and spread them over the soil. At least the garden was not far from the back of the house.

Then, and only then, was I able to get washed up and ready for school. My best dress was muddy and dirty so I wore my old dress on that first day at my new school. I went to school hungry as they never did give me permission to eat breakfast. Because we were late that first morning, Mr. Eigen gave me a ride to school. But after that I always had to walk, no matter how late I was.

When I got off the wagon at school, Mr. Eigen handed me a syrup pail. I figured it was my lunch. School had already started, and I was about 1½ hours late. My new brothers teased me all day about getting a ride to school when they had to walk. Poor things . . . they didn't have to do chores!

It was a small country school, and I was the only student in my grade. The teacher didn't seem happy to have me as she had no books nor any schoolwork set up for my grade. She pretty much ignored me the first week or so. I was often asked to join the higher grades in their discussions, though I really felt out of place. Everything was so cold and unforgiving. Even the kids seemed to have lost their ability to smile and interact with strangers like me.

The teacher seemed ever so strict. Everything was done with stern discipline—no talking except when we asked or answered a question or when we went outside for recess. I knew from the beginning that school was not going to be any fun.

Walking home after school took forever. I hurried as fast as I could, but the family just diddle-dawdled along at their leisure. Once home I was admonished to hurry and change for chores. It didn't take long for me to figure out the routine, and then Mr. Eigen told me I could do the chores alone from now on. He kept busy in the fields or in his workshop. I grew more and more dissatisfied with doing all the chores as I listened to the boys fight and argue with one another in the house. I could hear them all the way out in the barn.

When I finished with the barn chores, I headed to the house, changed clothes, and fixed supper as ordered by Mrs. Eigen. While the family ate, I changed back into my barn clothes to do the chicken and pig chores. When I finished, back to the house I'd go, change clothes again, and clean up the kitchen. I was allowed to eat my meal, if there was anything left. If not, I fixed crackers and milk in a glass for myself. Often I was asked to bake cookies or cake at night for the next day.

Eventually I asked permission to clean the kitchen floor in the evening instead of morning. This helped to shorten the routine so I wouldn't be so late for school. When the floor was clean, I was finally able to retreat to my room with a kerosene lamp, where I sat on the floor and did my homework. Later on that year, the Eigens told the teacher that I would be attending school only in the afternoons as I wasn't finishing my chores fast enough to attend morning classes.

Saturdays were the hardest days of all. That was the day I did clothes washing. That meant washing clothes for six people on a washboard and hanging the clothes on the line to dry. In the winter I would hang them on clotheslines strung up in the living room as well as on clothes bars. We had to walk around clothes hanging from the ceiling for days. I had to find time to iron all these clothes in addition to my other chores. I was instructed to dust the furniture in one room every day of the week. That meant I dusted the seven-room house every week. Every Saturday I would have to scrub and clean the outside toilet. Of course, there were always the three potties under the three beds to empty every morning.

Mrs. Eigen was constantly teaching Mary something about the piano, proper attire, or manners that involved eating or sitting. Also she was forever correcting Mary on her language skills, and she made her read book after book. I felt sorry for her at times. She seemed so stressed for such a young little girl. But one good thing was that Mrs. Eigen was gone much of the time to her gatherings and meetings at the church.

I was allowed to bathe only on Saturday evenings. Then I was given a clean dress, a clean pair of panties, socks, and special shoes to wear to church. After church I had to return the dress, socks, panties, and shoes for Mrs. Eigen to keep until the next week.

I lived in the old dresses I had brought from the orphanage throughout the week. Mrs. Eigen did give me fresh aprons to wear while I was working in the kitchen.

I never went with the family anywhere except to church, where I could visit with everyone as much as I liked. But once I got home, it was back to no talking immediately. I changed clothes, returned them to Mrs. Eigen, and fixed the Sunday meal. After eating, the family usually had some outing planned. They drove off in the buggy while I stayed behind to attend to the long list of extra chores they had written down for me.

These were the times when I thought about my siblings. I worried and cried, wondering where they were and how they were being treated. I tried writing to Edythe but never got any letters back. I wrote to the Faribault School too, but never heard from them either. I kept begging Mr. Eigen to take me to see them, but he always refused. I often had nightmares about Billy being hurt or sick.

I soon realized how distant I was from my family. No one probably even knew where I was. I felt terribly depressed and lonely most of the three years I was with the Eigen family. For a girl who often laughed and had a sense of humor, I never showed it to that uncaring family on that farm.

## *Chapter 25*
## *The Beating and the Schroht Family*

There was only one time that I remember being beaten by the Eigens. It happened one summer evening when I had just finished doing the kitchen floor after supper. I was carrying the ashes to the garden when the oldest boy grabbed my dustpan and ran with it back into the kitchen and dumped the ashes all over the clean kitchen floor. I was so upset and angry that I picked up the broom near the door, chased him around the yard until I cornered him near the chicken coop, and beat him on the back with it. Mr. Eigen watched all this and then proceeded to come at me. He grabbed the broom away from me and beat me twice as hard as I had hit his son. After the beating I was sent back into the kitchen to redo the floor. I had to stay home from school the next few days because I was black and blue with bruises. That was the first and last time I ever saw Mr. Eigen so angry. I believe that his stand was to defend his son and to put me in my place to remind me that I was nothing more then a servant-slave. I never allowed myself to feel close to this family after that incident.

Mrs. Eigen had a sister, Amelia, who lived on a nearby farm with her husband, Daniel Schroht, and their nine children. Amelia apparently realized how I was being treated so she often asked her sister if she could take me to her place once in a while on Sunday afternoons to play with her kids. We had a terrific time just being teenagers. There were five girls I made friends with: Hilda, Lillian, Florence, Gladys and Gloria. We talked and fooled around for hours. I hated to have the visit end because I knew what was waiting back at the Eigen farm.

On most Sundays I stayed home and worked "like the devil" to try and finish my list of chores before the Eigens came back from their outings. If I wasn't done with everything, I was sent to my room without supper but only after I had done all the evening chores. Then I had to clean the kitchen floor in the morning along with my usual list of household tasks before I was allowed to leave for school. And this, of course, was never until afternoon as I was not allowed to go in the mornings. I missed a lot of school and wonder now how I ever passed into the next grade. I graduated from the eighth grade while at the farm, and that was the extent of my schooling, which was the accepted level of education at this time.

*Sarah with three of the Schroht sisters: Hilda, Florence, Sarah, Gladys*

## *Chapter 26*
## *People, Buggies and the Auction*

One Sunday afternoon when I had finished my list of chores, I went to sit in the ditch that ran along the driveway of the farm. I was about 17 years old, lonely, and craved companionship. It was fun to simply watch folks drive by in their buggies filled with families and friends going who knows where. On this particular day, I noticed numerous buggies heading past me in the same direction, so I decided to follow them by running through the woods near the road that was used as a pasture for the cows. I ran about a mile or so when I came upon the neighboring farm crowded with people and buggies. They were having an auction, and the noise of the event sent my head whirling with all sorts of exciting thoughts.

People were everywhere, mulling around looking and talking with one another. I managed to find a seat by crawling up on a fence post in their cow pasture and wrapping my legs around it.

Two boys playing nearby noticed me sitting on the fence and started to tease me by throwing cow dung aimed in my direction. I was terrified and angry but didn't want to cause any trouble, so I jumped down and ran all the way home. I didn't want to have another episode with Mr. Eigen and the broom handle again. The boys followed me for a short distance but then gave up and went back.

The next Sunday I was sitting in the ditch again when I noticed a buggy coming down the road with two boys in it. I recognized them as the same two who had chased me the week before. They started to slow down to a stop so I jumped up and ran into the woods. I nearly outran them, but they caught up to me. I was terrified of what they might do. Thoughts came flooding back about what my own father had done to me when I was young. The boys managed to grab me and throw me to the ground, and with all my might I tried to fight them off to no avail.

The biggest boy held me down by sitting on my chest. He said, "Stop fighting and listen to me! I just wanted to come and tell you how sorry I am for throwing those cow pies at you last Sunday." He released me, stood up, and walked back to his buggy with his friend and left. I sat there for the longest time trying to make sense of it. Eventually I got up, dusted myself off, and walked back to the farm.

The Sunday after that baffling encounter, I was sitting alone in the ditch again when the same buggy showed up, only this time the boy was alone. He stopped in front of me and stepped down. The young man extended his hand and introduced himself as Edgar Sanborn and asked what my name was. The two of us sat in the ditch and talked the hour away. I found out he lived in the nearby village of Cannon City. He seemed like a very nice, caring, and compassionate young man, and my heart pounded with excitement when he asked me questions about myself. This was something no one had ever taken the time to do with me—ever! Here was a person interested in me and me alone. This was a totally new experience. I felt warm all over, and my heart was pounding so much that it almost jumped out of my chest.

Edgar came as often as he could on Sundays to visit me that summer. I confided in him all that had happened to me the past few years in the orphanage. I even told him that I had forgotten my glasses at the orphanage when I left. The next week he wrote a letter to the orphanage and asked them to send the glasses to my address at the farm. What a sweet thing for this young man to do just for me.

As our relationship grew, he became more and more concerned with my living situation as a servant-slave with the Eigens. He even asked me if I would ever consider leaving if he could find me a job of some sort elsewhere. I had always thought that there was no way out of my troubles. I knew I would become independent when I turned 18, but that was months away. I soon realized that I was falling in love with this man, Edgar. I was beginning to dream how I wanted to spend the rest of my life with him.

We started to plan how we would make arrangements for him to meet me one evening after dark in his buggy. I was elated to be planning how I was going to leave the farm. There was never a tear or even a good-bye. I only knew I was going to miss the fine friends that I had found with the Schroht family. Little did I know just how much the Schrohts would be involved in my life as time went on.

*The Schroht family and Sarah kept in touch all the rest of their lives. They were together when they married, and were godparents for each other's children. They often lived close enough to visit and socialize as a family when their kids were growing up. The Schrohts were always the first one to help when a crisis arose. Sarah personally adopted them as her family, and she felt they were her brothers and sisters, taking the place of her siblings who were taken from her.*

Edgar's sister, Pearl, found me a job working as a housemaid in the Twin Cities area. She was a few years older than Edgar and worked for a doctor there. She convinced him to have me come and help out. Pearl bought me a bus ticket, and Edgar brought it out to me one Sunday. When the opportunity presented itself, I sneaked out of the house late one night and walked along the road near the woods. He was waiting for me in his buggy and took me into Faribault. We waited there for the next bus to Minneapolis. He walked me to the door of the waiting bus and kissed me before I could say good-bye. This was the first time I had allowed him to kiss me. In fact, it was the first time I had ever been kissed by a boy. It was the most perfect moment in my entire life. So this was what love felt like!

Edgar had given me money to call Pearl on the phone when I got to Minneapolis. She sent a taxi down to the station to pick me up, and the driver took me to the address she had given me. Pearl greeted me with the biggest hug I had ever received, and she didn't really know me. This was the first time we had met. Already I felt like a queen who had just been lifted out of a dungeon. When I was taken to my own room that held a full-size bed that was just for me, I knew that things would be different here. I shared a bathroom, including a tub, with the two other maids (Pearl, the downstairs maid, and Ethyl, the upstairs maid). I was hired as the kitchen and dining room maid. For the first time ever in my life, I was able to fill the tub with warm, clean water and bathe alone for as long as I wanted. And to my amazement, I was given a fresh uniform, apron, and underclothes every day of the week.

When I had the required checkup by the doctor before I started work, I stood 4 feet 11½ inches tall and weighed 72 pounds. I was to report to the kitchen every day by 8 a.m. and help out until 5 p.m. For this work I was paid $5 per week. I felt as rich and privileged as the queen of England. The rest of the time was my own with some weekends off. Then Edgar would come to visit, or I traveled on the bus to Faribault to visit him. We would walk all over the town of Faribault, find a park and have a picnic that Edgar's mother had fixed for us.

**Edgar and Sally on their wedding day, June 21, 1930**

I turned 18 in March, and Edgar turned 19 in June, the same month we were married. The year was 1930. We had five children and spent 53½ years together before Edgar was called home to heaven in January of 1984 from a massive heart attack.

*Sally holding Arlene, Edgar, Paul and Eugene*

*Sally and Edgar's family in June of 1980, their Golden Anniversary*

# *Afterword*

*Eventually my mother, Sarah, wrote a letter to the orphanage letting them know where she was. She contacted them while working in Minneapolis later that same year. She never did contact the Eigens about her disappearance. By this time she had turned 18 so was no longer bound to the farm or to the orphanage.*

*It was a law that all orphans were to receive $100 from the state when they turned 18, so she wrote and asked for her money. She had just had an emergency appendectomy and needed to pay her hospital bill. She was never paid a single penny for her work with the Eigens. She informed everyone at this time that she never wanted to be called Sarah again and that she was changing her name to Sally. This was her way to put behind her all she had endured, leaving the past where it belonged. It was her way of healing. Until the day of her death, she wrote her name as Sally Sanborn. She never wore black shoes again in her life!*

*Edythe ran away from the orphanage at age 17. She married young and had three children. Eventually she divorced, and she married six times more. Edythe and Sally kept in touch often. They grew old being close friends as well as sisters. Edythe traveled all over the United States but always stayed in touch with Sally by writing letters.*

*Shortly after she was married, Sally went to the Faribault School for the Feeble Minded and Colony for Epileptics, as it was called then, to check on Billy. She learned that he had died on November 28, 1927, at age 12 of an infection caused by third degree burns on his face and body, according to the statement on the death certificate. She was living at the Eigen farm at the time, but she was never informed. Authorities wouldn't tell her where he had been laid to rest. All they said was that it was an unmarked grave, and they didn't have any information as to its location. She returned nearly every year to try to learn more but was told that the cemetery area had been turned into a ball field.*

*Three years before she passed away, she went once more and found that all the information had been put into a computer. The school administrator gave her Billy's records. Then he personally drove her to the cemetery and walked her to Billy's grave site. She stayed alone by the grave in a soft rain for nearly an hour praying and grieving. She had a headstone placed there to honor him, the first gravestone to be installed in this little cemetery. His records show that Billy had tried to run away at least two times but was caught and returned to the school.*

*After Violet left the Faribault School for the Deaf, Dumb and Blind, she hopped a freight train car filled with hoboes, homeless men riding the rails from town to town, trying to find work or food. One of the men, Clifford Dobson, realized Violet's vulnerability, took her under his wing and protected her from the sins of the world. They traveled together for a while and ended up in Brainerd, where they married. Clifford spent 48 years of married life providing for Violet by shoveling and delivering coal and, in later years, working as a garbage collector.*

*Violet had a hysterectomy when she was 12 years old, so Violet and Clifford never had any children, but their love for one another kept them together as lifelong soul mates. Violet had experimental surgery at age 8 to reverse her hearing loss. It actually worked and was successful in giving back some of her hearing. It was never perfect, but she always felt blessed just to be able to hear as well as she did. These experimental types of surgery were often tried on orphans. They were the perfect candidates as they supposedly had no parents and were declared wards of the state by the courts.*

*Violet made contact with Grandpa Green after her marriage. They remained close until his death. She then inherited the trunk of Caroline Cook Richards. She also received the trunk of Grandpa and Grandma Green. These trunks and some photographs are the only remnants of this family's life before they were separated and sent to state schools.*

After Sally had been married about 16 years, she located her sister Dorothy. She was living in Beloit, Wisconsin, with her husband and three children. Her mother had taken her as a baby to be raised with the help of her grandmother, Etta Schueman, near Rockton, Illinois. Sally went to visit her for the first time in 1946. They cried, hugged, and talked for hours trying to figure out how and why their lives had taken such different turns.

This was also the time when Sally met her mother for the first time since she walked away from that cabin so many years ago. There were hours of sobbing, tears, angry raised voices and a thousand questions. Eventually Caroline begged for forgiveness. Somehow, Sally found it in her heart to grant her request. I don't think Sally could ever forget what this woman did to her children by deserting them at their greatest time of need, but she did seem to find understanding for her mother's actions as she grew older. They kept a distant, cordial contact by mail and visited every couple of years or so until Caroline passed away.

Sally never saw her father again after he left to go to the Dakotas to earn all that money. She was informed by the State School of his death after she was married, but she didn't attend his funeral. She found out later where he was laid to rest, but she never visited his grave.

Sally spent her last years after her faithful husband, Edgar, passed away in 1984 by being devoted to her children, grandchildren, and great grandchildren until the time of her death at the age of 79 in 1991. She never lived more than 20 miles from the Owatonna State School Orphanage, but she didn't want to return to visit the site again. She looked the other way every time she had to go down that road.

One Sunday afternoon in 1989, when Sally was 77, I took her for a ride around Owatonna and spent an hour or so walking through Mineral Springs Park. She marveled at the growth of the park compared to her memories of that night so long ago when she came for water. We ended up in the parking lot of the orphanage. It was no longer an orphanage but is called the West Hills complex, now owned by the city of Owatonna. They were having an open house for the public. I told her

*I thought it was time for her to get the demons off her back and out of her heart. She broke down and sobbed, sitting there in the front seat of my car near the front door of the orphanage. She said it brought back a rush of the horrible feelings that she had endured when she was dragged up those front steps by those two strong men on October 8, 1925.*

*Eventually she got out with my help, walked up the steps through the front door, and entered the building. She stood in front of the opening going into the tower and cried some more. I led her onward through the dining hall and into the kitchen and dining room where she had served the professors and teachers. She meandered around the room feeling the wall and gazing intently at the floor, looking like she was trying to recognize something familiar. She stopped abruptly, turned around, and looked me square in the eye. She said, "I'll show you just what this place is all about!"*

*She took me by the elbow and led me out the back of the kitchen and down some steps. We walked to a hall (tunnel) where she stopped and searched at great lengths but eventually found the marks on the wall where the shackles had been. She ran her hand carefully over the filled-in spot, tears running down her cheeks, then turned to me and said softly, "Now YOU know!" She left quietly; then peacefully walked out the back kitchen door and down the sidewalk to the car. She never went back, and she never told me any more stories after that day.*

*I called her the evening before her fatal stroke and asked her what she was doing. She said that she had just put on her nightgown and was sitting at the kitchen table having her glass of crackers and milk before she went to bed.*

*And now you know her story. May God bless the memory of my mother, Sally (Sarah) Etta Richards Sanborn.*

*Edythe, Dorothy, & Sally,*
*1974 reunion*

*Edythe & Sally's last visit in 1990*
*Still arguing about carrot seeds*

*Violet, Caroline, Sally, Etta (sitting)*
*Second reunion with Caroline, 1955.*

*Arlene, Sarah, Caroline (back)*
*Pamela (Arlene's daughter), Etta*

*Pearl and her brother Edgar*

*40th Anniversary, 1970, Sally and Edgar*

**_Sally (Sarah) Etta Richards Sanborn, 1980_**

_Thanks, Mom, for the memories. Without your courage to come forth and share these stories, which started the healing process, I could not have written this book. I will love your forever and a day!   Arlene_